P9-AFN-836

Provence Interiors
Intérieurs de Provence

Lisa Lovatt-Smith

Provence Interiors
Intérieurs de Provence

Edited by | Sous la direction de | Herausgegeben von
Angelika Muthesius

TASCHEN

KÖLN LONDON LOS ANGELES MADRID PARIS TOKYO

Couverture / Front cover / Umschlagvorderseite:
Un mas de campagne près de Tarascon (voir pp. 98–103)
A rural "mas" not far from Tarascon (see pp. 98–103)
Ein bäuerlicher »mas« in der Nähe von Tarascon (s. S. 98–103)
Décoration / Decoration / Gestaltung: Marie Steinberg, Paris
Photo: Guillaume de Laubier

Dos de couverture / Back cover / Umschlagrückseite:
Jardin du Domaine de Souviou (voir pp. 246–255)
Garden of the property "Domaine de Souviou" (see pp. 246–255)
Garten des Anwesens »Domaine de Souviou« (s. S. 246–255)
Photo: Jérôme Darblay

Reproduction page 2 / Illustration page 2 / Abbildung Seite 2:
Détail dans la maison de Nicole de Vesian (voir pp. 162–173)
A detail in the home of Nicole de Vesian (see pp. 162–173)
Detail im Haus von Nicole de Vesian (s. S. 162–173)
Photo: Pascal Chevallier/TOP

Pages de garde / Endpaper / Vorsatzpapier:
Dessin de / Drawing by / Zeichnung von Hervé van der Straeten

To stay informed about upcoming TASCHEN titles, please request our magazine at
www.taschen.com or write to TASCHEN, Hohenzollernring 53, D-50672 Cologne, Germany,
Fax: +49-221-254919. We will be happy to send you a free copy of our magazine which is filled
with information about all of our books.

© 2004 TASCHEN GmbH
Hohenzollernring 53, D-50672 Köln
www.taschen.com
Original edition: © 1996 Benedikt Taschen Verlag GmbH
Edited and designed by Angelika Muthesius, Cologne
Text edited by Jutta Hendricks, Cologne
French translation by Philippe Safavi, Paris
English translation by Gillian Boughey, Paris (pp. 8–21)
German translation by Birgit Lamerz-Beckschäfer, Datteln, and
Hinrich Schmidt-Henkel, Hamburg (pp. 8–21)

Printed in Italy
ISBN 3-8228-3476-9

Sommaire
Contents
Inhalt

Une maison de rêve en Provence

Préface de Christian Lacroix
Photographies d'Edouard Boubat / TOP

The Provençal Dream House

Preface by Christian Lacroix
Photographs by Edouard Boubat / TOP

Ein Traumhaus in der Provence

Vorwort von Christian Lacroix
Photographien von Edouard Boubat / TOP

Houses in Provence are today's castles in the air. People hunt them as Tartarin hunted the lion, pursue them as they might Daudet's Arlésienne; they are precise as images, and yet are as hazy as the mirages that the dog-days set floating over the horizons of the Agachole beaches, between the pine groves and Atlantis. This hunt is mine too. My head full of fragments of the past and scraps of the future, I live in expectation of my house in Provence, which will, when time and place provide, prove the more perfect for every hesitation on the way. This vision will be the final piece in a jigsaw puzzle of childhood and adolescent memories, for "we build the future by enlarging upon the past" (Goethe).

For ten years, this "patch-work" has served my aspiration to create the fashions of today; tomorrow it will serve a return to my roots. The Mediterranean is a magnet. Its siren song is heard in New York, London and Paris; all of them find themselves at home there, and with every new recruit it feels itself still more the capital, the cradle, the centre of the world. Its magnetism was never so strongly felt as when I tore myself from the Midi to "go up to Paris"; even now, in Saint-Germain-des-Prés where we live, its influence remains and it is the bold, grand, amiable façades of Aix, Arles or Montpellier town houses that I seek. Our Left Bank apartment wears the blood-red and old-gold livery of Spain and Provence; the Lacroix "Maison de Couture" on the Right Bank, with its terracotta, bare wood and bronzed ironwork is an Embassy of the Camargue in the centre of Faubourg Saint-Honoré. With every new day, we build upon the foundations of yesterday: the sediment of imagery laid down by the past.

As a child, I honed my imagination on the birth of humanity, dreaming of a troglodytic life in the Val d'Enfer. December's *Pastorales* told us the same story, those 19th-century plays in Provençal that recounted the nativity through the folkloric characters of the South, characters also found in the crib. Where was the Christ-child born, if not here in the Alpilles? The nativity unfolds amid the timbers and straw of the stable, the bare rocks of the landscape, the 18th-century Indian silks of the players. In short, the last word in Provençal decoration is al-

Les maisons en Provence sont les châteaux en Espagne d'aujourd'hui. On les chasse comme Tartarin chassait le lion, on les poursuit comme «l'Arlésienne», vagues et précises, images-mirages ondoyantes que la canicule génère à l'horizon des plages de l'Agachole, entre Atlantide et pinèdes vierges. Moi le premier, car ma maison en Provence je l'attends encore, la tête pleine de «pans» de passé, de «parcelles» d'à venir, reculant tellement que le saut ne devrait en être que plus que parfait, le lieu et le moment venus. Cet idéal sera l'achèvement d'un puzzle fabriqué à partir de tant d'impressions d'enfant et d'adolescent puisque nous «bâtissons le futur avec les éléments élargis du passé» (Goethe).

Ce travail de «patchs» que je fais depuis presque dix ans en tâchant de confectionner les modes d'aujourd'hui, je l'appliquerai à ce retour au bercail. La Méditerranée est un aimant. Ses Sirènes ont toujours fasciné de leurs chants, New-York, Londres et Paris qui s'y sentent chez eux, la faisant ainsi se sentir davantage encore capitale, nombril, berceau du monde. Son attraction magnétique s'est exercée de toutes ses forces, lorsqu'il s'est agi de m'arracher au Midi pour «monter à Paris» où son empreinte reste si vivace que dans Saint-Germain-des-Prés où nous vivons, ce sont les «fronts» aussi «audacieux» qu'aimables des hôtels aixois, arlésiens ou montpelliérains que je cherche. Et si, Rive Gauche, notre appartement a le sang séché et l'or vieilli d'Espagne et de Provence, la Maison de Couture a, Rive Droite, les terres cuites, les bois sauvages et les fers patinés d'une Ambassade de Camargue en plein Faubourg Saint-Honoré. On ne bâtit chaque jour et les suivants que sur les fondations, tout en images stratifiées, d'hier.

Enfant, c'était la naissance de l'humanité qui exacerbait mon imagination dans le Val d'Enfer où je me rêvais troglodyte. Pour nous, c'est ce que nous racontaient en décembre les Pastorales, (pièces de théâtre XIXe en provençal, mettant en scène la nativité uniquement avec des types populaires méridionaux que l'on retrouve parmi les personnages des santons): L'Enfant-Jésus n'avait pu naître que quelque part dans les Alpilles. Paille et poutre de l'étable, rochers bruts du paysage, étoffes indiennes

Die Häuser der Provence sind die Luftschlösser der heutigen Zeit. Wir jagen ihnen nach wie Tartarin de Tarascon – der provenzalische Don Quijote im Roman von Alphonse Daudet – seinem unerreichbaren Löwen. Immer sind sie greifbar, doch schon wieder fort, sind flüchtig und beständig zugleich, wie eine Fata Morgana flimmern sie in der glühenden Hitze am Horizont der Strände von L'Agachole, zwischen Atlantis und Piniendschungel. Auch ich habe mein Ideal eines Hauses in der Provence noch nicht gefunden; zu sehr schwirrt mir der Kopf von Splittern der Vergangenheit und Orten der Zukunft. Ich nehme sehr großen Anlauf, so daß der Sprung am Ende, wenn Ort und Zeit endlich stimmen, mehr als vollkommen sein dürfte. Sollte ich dieses Ideal jemals erreichen, dann wird es die Vollendung eines Puzzles aus tausenderlei Kindheits- und Jugenderinnerungen sein, bauen wir doch alle »ein ewig Neues, das sich aus den erweiterten Elementen des Vergangenen gestaltet« (Goethe).

Das Patchwork, an dem ich seit fast zehn Jahren arbeite – indem ich versuche, die Moden von heute zu schneidern – wird auch diese Rückkehr zu den Wurzeln bestimmen. Das Mittelmeer ist ein Magnet. Seine Sirenen locken seit jeher mit ihren Gesängen; New York, London und Paris fühlen sich an ihm gleichermaßen zu Hause und sorgen dafür, daß es sich selber immer mehr als Hauptstadt, Nabel und Wiege der Welt begreift. Als ich wehmütig den Süden Frankreichs verließ, um nach Paris zu gehen, hat mich die Faszination des Mediterranen bis nach Saint-Germain-des-Prés verfolgt, wo wir wohnen: Immer noch halte ich hier Ausschau nach den ebenso kühnen wie anmutigen Giebeln der Stadthäuser von Aix-en-Provence, Arles oder Montpellier. Die Farben unserer Wohnung auf der Rive Gauche sind Altgold und getrocknetes Blut wie in Spanien oder der Provence, und die Maison de Couture auf der Rive Droite ist voller Terrakotta, rohem Holz und patiniertem Eisen, als wäre das Haus eine Gesandtschaft der Camargue mitten im Faubourg Saint-Honoré. Wir bauen schließlich nicht alle Tage, und wenn, dann errichten wir unsere Häuser als Nachkommen: Ihre Fundamente sind die geschichteten Bilder des Gestern.

ready set forth in cradle and crib. Provence was a time machine that delivered us to the life and architecture of the past. We could see ourselves as Greek or Roman in the ruins of Glanum, our Provençal Pompeii outside Saint-Rémy, or on the terraces of the ancient theatres and amphitheatres. Statues enrobed or erotic, miraculous columns, exquisite mosaics were the stuff of everyday. The sarcophagi of the Alyscamps offered us funeral prospects of epic grandeur. We lived amid the pages of history, learning Latin and Greek so as to decipher them in the medieval streets, Renaissance palace façades quarried from the amphitheatre and pre-Revolutionary churches that have now been turned into museums of pagan art. The distant past was sunlight in the street or sealed into the shadows of the Museon Arlaten – which no-one should settle in Provence, nor attempt the least construction, renovation or decoration, without having visited.

The Camargue
The beginning of the World was Les Saintes-Maries-de-la-Mer, where wind beat wave on saline earth: reed-built huts, fishermen's tiny cottages, and the serpentine lengths of limewashed *mas*, whose blue delta shutters strangely echoed the Ile de Ré. Immaculate, sparsely furnished interiors had no decoration but what work and life required: copper, leather, horsehair. Fabric in broad navy chequers. Wrought iron, stuffed birds, photos and pictures by local artists were post-war invaders of this ascetic, aristocratic, almost primitive simplicity. Till then, mistral, marshland and mosquito barred all but the true devotees of the flickering light of the paraffin lamp.

Until the sixties, it felt like some pampas land of the literary imagination; windmills on the horizon; apathetic, crumbling villages amid the dust of beaten earth; precarious, heteroclite dwellings built of driftwood, scrap iron, reinforced-concrete leftovers. The ponds in mother-of-pearl or violet, the geometric patterns of the sun-cracked earth, the ink-black mud of the marshland, the blood-orange sunsets and the salmon-pink flamingos reflected in dark water – all this made up the exotic poetry of that

XVIIIe des personnages; tous les éléments de la décoration provençale «dernier cri» sont déjà dans la crèche. La machine à remonter et visiter le temps et l'architecture n'avait plus qu'à se mettre en branle. Nous pouvions nous croire grecs ou romains dans les fouilles de Glanum (équivalent d'Herculanum et Pompéi à côté de Saint-Rémy) comme sur les gradins des théâtres antiques ou des arènes. Statues lascives ou drapées, colonnes miraculeuses, mosaïques recherchées étaient notre quotidien et les sarcophages des Alyscamps laissaient présager un au-delà épique; nous vivions dans les pages des livres d'histoire, apprenant grec et latin pour mieux les déchiffrer dans les rues médiévales, le long des Palais Renaissance construits avec les pierres de l'Amphithéâtre ou dans les églises d'avant la Révolution transformées en musées d'art païen. La nuit des temps était en plein jour ou à l'ombre fraîche du «Museon Arlaten» que quiconque, ayant le projet d'installer ses pénates quelque part par là, se doit de visiter avant de tenter le moindre geste de construction, rénovation ou décoration.

La Camargue
Quant au commencement du Monde, c'était Les Saintes-Maries-de-la-Mer: le vent, les vagues et la terre salée s'y confondent; cabanes en «sagne» (roseaux), minuscules maisons de pêcheurs ou longs reptiles des mas blanchis à la chaux à volets bleus jumelant étrangement le Delta avec l'Ile de Ré, intérieurs essentiels, immaculés, meubles rares et sombres, toiles à grands carreaux marines, avec pour seule décoration les outils et ustensiles des travaux et des jours, cuivre, cuir et crin de cheval. Le fer forgé, les oiseaux naturalisés et des photos ou tableaux d'artistes locaux ont seuls entamé, après-guerre, le primitivisme ascétique et aristocratique de ces demeures restées authentiques un peu par force. Le mistral, les marécages et les moustiques ne laissent pénétrer que les amoureux véritables à la lueur des lampes à pétrole.

Jusqu'aux années soixante, je m'y croyais dans des pampas de littérature avec les éoliennes à l'horizon, les hameaux lézardant, apathiques dans la poussière des terres battues et les baraques pré-

Als Kind entzündete sich meine Phantasie an Träumen von der Frühzeit des Menschen; ich träumte von mir selbst als Höhlenbewohner im Val d'Enfer, dem »Höllental« zu Füßen von Les-Baux-de-Provence. Ähnlich wirkten auf uns Kinder die »Pastorales«, jene aus dem 19. Jahrhundert stammenden Theaterstücke in provenzalischer Sprache, in denen die Weihnachtsgeschichte ausschließlich mit volkstümlichen Charakteren des Südens dargestellt wird: Das Jesuskind war also irgendwo in den Alpilles zur Welt gekommen, daran bestand kein Zweifel. Stroh und Holzträger, unbearbeitetes Felsgestein der Gegend, die indischen Stoffe aus dem 18. Jahrhundert, aus denen die Kostüme geschneidert waren: Schon in unseren Krippen damals war alles vorhanden, was jetzt als »letzter Schrei« der typisch provenzalischen Dekoration gilt. Die Zeitmaschine, die uns in die Vergangenheit der Menschen und der Architektur entführte, lief perfekt. In den Ausgrabungen von Glanum – den Resten einer römischen Stadt bei Saint-Rémy-de-Provence – und auf den Stufen der antiken Amphitheater konnten wir uns als alte Griechen oder Römer fühlen. Statuen von lasziven oder in Gewänder drapierten Gestalten, elegante Säulen und kunstreiche Mosaiken waren für uns ein alltäglicher Anblick, und die Sarkophage von Les Alyscamps, der großen römischen Nekropole in Arles, ließen ein episches Jenseits erahnen; wir lebten inmitten der geschichtlichen Zeugnisse, lernten Griechisch und Latein, um die Inschriften in den mittelalterlichen Straßen besser entziffern zu können, an den Fassaden der Renaissance-Gebäude, die mit den Steinen des Amphitheaters gebaut waren, oder an den Kirchen aus der Zeit vor der Revolution, die nun Museen heidnischer Kunst beherbergen. Im »Museon Arlaten« in Arles, das jeder besuchen muß, bevor er sich in dieser Gegend niederläßt, bevor er baut, ja selbst, bevor er an Renovierung oder Ausschmückung auch nur denkt, liegt die dunkle Vergangenheit in hellem Licht oder zumindest in kühlem Halbschatten.

Die Camargue
Der Anbeginn der Welt aber lag für uns in Les Saintes-Maries-de-la-Mer, wo Wind, Wellen und salzige

closed and singular world of the *bouvine*, the breeders of bull and horse. Those that played in the "jet set" of the time, brought to this natural austerity incongruous neo-gothic objects, modern furniture or the sophistication of a botanical garden.

Summer in Fontvieille, Winter in Arles

White horses, black bulls and the neutral tones of the vegetation imparted a "zen" simplicity to the severity and abstraction of these houses that contrasted with the polychrome kitsch of the gypsy caravans and the more sensual inviting opulence of Fontvieille where we would spend June. This was the country not of Baroncelli but Pagnol: from the *pâtissier's* oven wafted the scent of marshmallow, the shelves of the bookshop were redolent of fresh-printed ink and the streams ran laundry blue. Pine, lavender and thyme masked every other fragrance. The quarries gave a pale blond stone like that of Aix and the prosperous villages, with their pergolas of wisteria and trellises loaded with vines, coiled snugly beneath the plane trees that lined their alleys. Inside, monochrome drawings in ochre, larkspur or pistachio embellished the lower half of the walls. Shutters were painted the same slightly *gauloise* blue as the carts or green like the garden furniture before white established itself as the supreme elegance. Visitors were received under the bowers – as in the Marseille *cabanons*, the *masets* of Nîmes or the mountain solitudes of Perpignan – amid a profusion of wicker, carafes and bottles. In summer, the perfume of the fig trees, a musk-like, milky fragrance, prevailed over all others, while the acrid geraniums overflowed from oil or olive jars of all shapes and sizes. Carnations and iris were planted at street level, and the pavements in Crau stone ran beneath façades in which the doors were closed behind one by a pulley weighted with a little cotton bag full of sand; they opened onto heavy-fringed anti-mosquito mesh, later replaced by the multi-coloured plastic-strip curtains of the fifties and sixties.

The same little groups gathered in winter around fires perfumed by clementines, cloves and old wine. There was the respectable sensuality of Fourques furniture all in curves and arabesques,

caires, hétéroclites, en bois flottés, ferrailles de récupération, vestiges de béton armé. Les étangs nacrés ou violacés, le sol séché en craquelures géométriques ou la vase des marais couleur d'encre, les couchers de soleil «orange sanguine» et le rose saumoné des flamants qu'ils reflétaient étaient pour beaucoup dans l'exotique poésie de ces lieux abritant l'univers très fermé et particulier de la «Bouvine» (élevage de taureaux et de chevaux). Certains faisaient le lien avec la «jet-society» de l'époque, apportant à cette austérité naturelle la touche décalée d'objets néo-gothiques, de meubles «modern style» ou la sophistication d'un jardin botanique.

L'été en Fontvieille, l'hiver en Arles

Blanc des chevaux, noir des taureaux, non-couleur des végétaux donnaient le ton «zen», abstrait et sévère de ces maisons sans fioritures, en contraste avec le kitsch polychrome des roulottes de gitans et l'opulence plus charnelle, souriante et avenante de Fontvieille où nous passions juin. Là ce n'était plus Baroncelli mais Pagnol, le four du pâtissier exhalait un arôme de guimauve, les étals du libraire avaient une odeur d'imprimerie humide et les ruisseaux emportaient l'eau bleue des lessives; mais par-dessus tout, les pins, le thym et la lavande dominaient implacablement. La pierre des carrières possédait un peu de la blondeur aixoise et ces villages cossus se lovaient en rond sous des allées de platanes, des treilles de vigne vierge, ou des pergolas de glycines. A l'intérieur, les murs jouaient les soubassements en camaïeux d'ocres, de bleus «Sainte Vierge» ou de pistache. Les persiennes étaient du même azur un peu «gauloise» dont on peignait les charrettes, du vert des meubles de jardin avant que le blanc ne devienne la suprême élégance. On recevait sous les tonnelles dans un désordre d'osier, de carafes et de bouteilles comme le dimanche dans les «cabanons» marseillais, les «campagnes» et les «masets» des environs de Nîmes ou même les «solitudes» des hauteurs de Perpignan. Les figuiers au gros des chaleurs le disputaient en fragrance à tout le reste avec une senteur particulière musquée et laiteuse tandis que les géraniums âcres dégoulinaient de toutes sortes de jarres à huile ou à olives. Des œillets et

Erde sich mischen, wo die mit Schilfrohr gedeckten Hütten, die winzigen Fischerkaten und die langgestreckten Reptilien der weißgekalkten »Mas« – der Landhäuser – auf eigenartige Weise mitten im Rhône-Delta an die Ile de Ré erinnern. Auf das Wesentlichste beschränkte Interieurs, düstere, kostbare Möbelstücke, große, weiß-blau karierte Tücher, dazu als einziger Schmuck das Tag für Tag benutzte Werkzeug und das Material, aus dem es gefertigt war, Kupfer, Leder, Roßhaar. Erst nach dem Zweiten Weltkrieg haben Ziergegenstände aus Schmiedeeisen, ausgestopfte Vögel und Fotos oder Bilder der lokalen Künstler die asketisch-aristokratische Kargheit dieser Häuser gebrochen, die aufgrund der äußeren Bedingungen bis dahin unberührt geblieben waren: Schließlich halten Mistral, Mücken und Sümpfe alle fern, außer denen, die es als wirkliche Liebhaber nicht scheuen, beim Licht der Petroleumlampen zu sitzen.

Bis in die sechziger Jahre hinein glaubte ich, mich hier inmitten einer aus der Literatur stammenden Pampa zu befinden, mit den windgetriebenen Schöpfpumpen am Horizont, den in der Sonne brütenden Weilern, apathisch unter dem Staub der gestampften Erde, und den bunt hingestreuten Hütten, gebaut aus Holz, das mit Flößen herbeigeschafft wurde, aus Metallschrott und aus Bruchstücken von armiertem Beton. Die perlmuttfarbenen oder violett schimmernden Seen, der zu geometrischen Mustern zersprungene, ausgetrocknete Boden oder der tintendunkle Schlamm, das blutige Orange der untergehenden Sonne und davor das Lachsrosa der Flamingos – all das gehörte für viele zur exotischen Poesie dieses abgeschlossenen, eigentümlichen Universums der »Bouvine«, der Stier- und Pferdezüchter, von denen manche Kontakt zum damaligen »Jet-set« hatten, so daß bald allerlei Importe in diese natürliche Düsterkeit einbrachen: neogothischer Nippes, Jugendstilmöbel oder – Gipfel des Snobismus – ein botanischer Garten.

Sommer in Fontvieille, Winter in Arles
Das Weiß der Pferde, das Schwarz der Stiere, die Blässe der Gewächse bildeten den »zen-haften«, abstrakten, strengen Grundton dieser schnörkellosen

holy images, starchy portraits, red tiles (*mallons*) underfoot, old stoneware sinks, pools of yellow light, cracked faïence, the mellow ticking of a clock. Everything that has since turned to gold in the hands of the antique merchant was then the stuff of everyday life. *Aficionados* of the bull-ring would indulge themselves with salons of a tauromachic baroque: capes, swords, banderillas and other trophies or relics. The thirties and forties added a zest of solid art deco, the tubby "club" armchair and vast wireless sets. Then the northern fashion for chintz was translated to the south in the form of serially coordinated countryfied cretonnes. A return to the town, where over the tangle of tiled roofs, belvederes and covered or glazed terraces that lines the banks of the Rhône, the horizon is dogtoothed with the limestone belltowers of Arles. Between the 17th and 19th century, houses had retained the often dismal half-dark of Raspal's paintings. Bare stone walls, occasional wainscoting with canvases sometimes pasted directly on to it; the occasional fresco. Paintings black with varnish, lanterns, the furniture of several different generations commingled, sometimes a music room long forgotten behind the penumbra of closed shutters, wide staircases with sinuous wrought-iron balustrades, a certain silence, the certainty of cold. Behind high walls were the hanging gardens with their labyrinthine terraces of trees, damp patches in plenty, a palm tree here, a palm tree there. Ivy, cretonne prints and the trimmings and braids of the fifties and sixties retained some measure of dignity, a certain lofty elegance. The seventies and eighties took a knife to these soft, upholstered, enclosed spaces, bastardized the complexity of volute and scroll, stripped façades to the bone, whitewashed them, rendered the pebble-dash sickly with the obligatory "peach", "almond" and "vanilla", transformed the ground floors into aquariums open to every eye, converted the *souillardes* (sculleries) into "loft / kitchenette / bistrot", and turned the surrounding land into appalling housing estates whose "inspiration" was ignorance, greed or a half-digested modernism.

My nostalgia is not obsessive. I am thrilled by contemporary architecture of talent. It is no less

des iris étaient plantés à même les rues, les trottoirs en «calade» (pierre) de Crau, à l'aplomb des façades qui s'ouvraient de portes à moustiquaires qu'un petit sac de cotonnade lesté de sable au bout d'un cordon à poulie, refermait en jouant les contre-poids, sur des rideaux en lourd filet frangés, plus tard remplacés par les lanières de plastique multicolores des années cinquante et soixante.

Les mêmes cénacles se réunissaient l'hiver au coin des cheminées qui embaumaient la clémentine, le clou de girofle et le vin vieux. Sensualité respectable des meubles de Fourques tout en courbes et arabesques, images saintes, portraits empesés, «mallons» (carreaux) rouges par terre, «pile» (évier) profonde de grès antique, éclairages jaunes un peu chiches, faïences craquelées, tic-tac d'horloge moelleux, fleurs et couleurs des boutis: tout ce répertoire devenu depuis l'or des marchands se vivait au jour le jour. Les aficionados risquaient le baroque d'un salon tauromachique accroché de têtes de «toros», capes, épées, banderilles et autres trophées ou reliques. Les années trente et quarante agrémentèrent ces décors d'un zeste d'Art déco massif, de fauteuils de cuir «club» et d'énormes postes de T.S.F. Puis la mode du chintz, au nord, se traduisit dans le sud par une marée de cretonnes folkloriques coordonnées à l'infini. Retour en ville, avec, à l'horizon, la mâchoire calcaire des clochers arlésiens étalés le long du Rhône dans l'enchevêtrement des toitures de tuiles, des belvédères et des terrasses couvertes ou vitrées. Les maisons XVIIe – XVIIIe et XIXe avaient gardé la pénombre pas forcément gaie des tableaux de Raspal. Murs de pierre nue, à peine quelques lambris ou toiles marouflées, fresques parfois. Des tableaux noircis de vernis, des lanternes, la coexistence des mobiliers de plusieurs générations et même un salon de musique oublié dans l'obscurité, d'amples escaliers à ferronneries sinueuses, un certain silence et un froid certain, des arbres sur des terrasses suspendues en labyrinthes derrière de hauts murs, beaucoup de taches d'humidité, souvent un palmier. Le lierre, la toile de Jouy et les passementeries des années cinquante et soixante avaient conservé une certaine réserve, encore un peu de hauteur et d'élégance. Puis les années

Häuser. Welch ein Kontrast zum vielfarbigen Kitsch der Zigeunerkarren, der »roulottes«, und der sinnlicheren, freundlicheren Opulenz des liebenswürdigen Örtchens Fontvieille, wo wir den Juni zu verbringen pflegten, im Reich der realistisch-idyllischen Geschichten des Schriftstellers und Filmers Marcel Pagnol (und nicht in der versponnen romantischen Provence des Epikers Baroncelli). Hier duftete es süß aus dem Ofen des Bäckers, der Stand des Buchhändlers roch nach feuchter Druckerschwärze, und die Bäche trugen bläuliche Waschlauge fort; alles jedoch war beherrscht von Pinien, Lavendel und Thymian. Die Steine aus den hiesigen Brüchen waren fast so hell wie diejenigen aus Aix, und die stämmigen Dörfer duckten sich unter Platanenalleen, unter Spalieren von wildem Wein und Pergolen voller Glyzinien. Drinnen massige Mauern, einfarbig ockergelb, blau – in einem »Sainte Vierge« genannten Ton – oder pistaziengrün. Die Fensterläden in demselben, etwas an Gauloise-Schachteln erinnernden Hellblau wie der Anstrich der Karren oder in dem Grün, in dem die Gartenmöbel gehalten waren, bevor Weiß als eleganteste Lösung aufkam. Unter den Gewölben empfing man seine Gäste in einem Durcheinander aus Korbmöbeln, Karaffen und Flaschen, ganz wie es an den Sonntagen in den ländlichen Häusern üblich war, den »Cabanons« in der Gegend von Marseille, den »Campagnes« und »Masets« rings um Nîmes oder gar den »Solitudes« auf den einsamen Höhen über Perpignan. In der größten Hitze versuchten die Feigensträucher, allem anderen den Rang abzulaufen, mit ihrem ganz besonderen moschusartigen, milchigen Duft, während aus zu Pflanzgefäßen verwandelten Öl- oder Olivenkübeln Geranien hingen. Nelken und Iris pflanzte man einfach an die Straße oder auf die Bürgersteige – diese waren aus Feldsteinen gesetzt – oder direkt an die Fassaden der Häuser. Als Eingangstür hatte man sommers Fliegengitter, die von einem kleinen, sandgefüllten Baumwollsäckchen zugezogen wurden, es hing als Gegengewicht an einem Strick, der über eine Rolle lief; drinnen Türvorhänge aus schwerem Netzgewebe mit Fransen, das später, in den Fünfzigern und Sechzigern, durch grellbunte Plastikstreifen verdrängt wurde.

soul-destroying to cut oneself off from one's memory than to wall oneself into a sterile and dogmatic tradition of regionalism. When, in 1987, I founded my "Maison de Couture", drawing on my roots to do so, to the rhythm of the Spanish *movida* I was inching open the gate of a secret garden where the music of the Gypsy Kings played. Since then I have often been tempted – pretension or presumption – to think of myself (and not just myself) as a sort of sorcerer's apprentice from whom flowed a tide of fashion that fashion itself made unfashionable. I had walked the soil of Provence to Paris and now Paris was at my coat-tails when I returned to my most intimate landmarks. I had forgotten that "the decisive event cannot be forestalled"; that I was myself carried on that tide, more instrument than *agent provocateur*. So I beat a retreat. My House in the South is a hotel in Arles (the Hôtel du Nord!), my Provence is really the Languedoc and my Camargue is the Petite Camargue on the fringes of my ancestral Cévennes. For now, my Paris is an ivory tower, an observatory from which to observe the year 2000, the Rhône valley and a few supplementary "flashcards": a Pagnolesque *Château de ma mère* – a sort of rustic, Napoléon III style Trianon full of opaline hues – next to Daudet's windmill, the interiors of Christian Bérard, a little hut on stilts, another amongst the trees of Aigues-Mortes, some 16th-century apartments at Baux with their successive terraced gardens, the naive paintings found in café-restaurants, the raw architecture, now endangered, of the Beauduc beachhouses, the Palladian villa in Lambese whose American owner lives, eats and dresses *à la* 18th century, and certain bourgeois residences in the parodic style of Tati. And I recall a succulent property imbued with the arty culture of its British inhabitants who had shown much more respect for it than did the native worthies who succeeded them. The beautiful gardens of Provence are almost always Anglo-Saxon. This is tradition: the Comtat Venaissin, antechamber to Tuscany. For Provence, like England or Italy, possesses the true and original aristocracy, the nobility of land, where the city counts for little. It is a rural, poetic, peasant civilisation remote from salons, out of reach of Parisian or Bovaryiste

snob-soixante-dix et quatre-vingt ont éventré la chair des volumes cloisonnés, abâtardi les circonvolutions complexes, mis à nu, à vif, à blanc les façades ou affadi les crépis avec la gamme obligatoire des «pêche», «amande» et «vanille», transformé les rez-de-chaussée en aquarium, les «souillardes» (arrière-cuisine) en «loft /kitchenette/bistrot», les alentours en lotissements désespérants pour cause d'ignorance, de lucre, ou de modernisme mal digéré.

Je ne suis pas d'une nostalgie pathologique. L'architecture contemporaine m'emballe quand elle a du talent. Et je pense qu'il y a autant de risque à perdre son âme avec sa mémoire, qu'à se retrancher dans le camp stérile du traditionalisme régionaliste. En 1987, au moment de fonder une Maison de Couture sur les bases de mes racines, j'ai entrouvert le portail d'un jardin secret sur la musique des Gypsy Kings et au même rythme que la Movida espagnole; j'ai été depuis souvent tenté d'avoir la prétention ou la présomption de me penser avec d'autres l'apprenti sorcier d'une mode déferlante vite démodable. J'avais charrié la Provence à mes semelles jusqu'à Paris et je traînais en retour Paris à mes basques jusqu'au fin fond de mes repères. C'était oublier que «ce qui est décisif se produit malgré tout» et que j'étais moi-même porté par une vague inéluctable, instrument plus qu'agent provocateur. Alors j'ai battu en retraite. Ma Maison dans le Sud est un hôtel à Arles («l'hôtel du Nord!»), ma Provence, c'est plutôt le Languedoc et ma Camargue, la «Petite» aux limites des Cévennes paternelles. Quant à mon Paris, pour un temps, c'est une tour d'ivoire ou plutôt un observatoire d'où scruter l'an 2000, la vallée du Rhône et quelques «flashes» supplémentaires: un «Château de ma mère», Trianon rustique et le style Napoléon III plein d'opalines à côté du Moulin de Daudet, et les intérieurs de Christian Bérard, une cabane sur pilotis et une autre dans les arbres à Aigues-Mortes, des appartements XVIe aux Baux, avec des jardins en cascade, des cafés-restaurants aux peintures naïves, l'art brut des constructions menacées sur la plage de Beauduc, la villa palladienne de Lambesc où une Américaine vit, mange et s'habille XVIIIe, les résidences à la Tati d'une certaine bourgeoisie. Je me souviens aussi

Im Winter dann fand man sich beim Kamin
zusammen, wo es nach Clementinen, Nelkengewürz
und altem Wein duftete. Dort war alles vereint, wo-
mit man heute für viel Geld Häuser einrichtet: Die
respektheischende Sinnlichkeit der Fourques-Möbel,
gewundene Arabesken, Heiligenbilder, steife Por-
träts, am Boden rote Terrakotta, an der Wand tiefe,
alte Steinzeug-Schüttsteine, dazu gelbliche, etwas
trübe Beleuchtung, Fayence-Keramik, dumpf
tickende Standuhren, Blumen und erdige Farben...
Begeisterte Stierkampfanhänger leisteten sich recht
barock anmutende Wohnzimmer voller ausgestopf-
ter Köpfe der »toros«, voller Capes, Schwerter, Banderillas und anderer Trophäen oder Reliquien. Die
dreißiger und vierziger Jahre würzten dieses Dekor
mit einer Prise massiver Art deco, mit ledernen
»Clubsesseln« und enormen Rundfunkgeräten. Da-
nach schwappte die Chintz-Welle aus dem Norden
in den Süden über und bescherte ihm eine Flut auf-
einander abgestimmter Kretonne-Folklorestoffe.

Bei der Rückkehr in die Stadt stieg dann am
Horizont entlang der Rhône das steinerne Gebiß der
Türme von Arles auf, das Gewirr von Ziegeldächern,
Erkern und überdachten oder verglasten Terrassen.
Die Häuser aus dem 17., 18. und dem 19. Jahrhundert strahlten die nicht gerade fröhliche Düsterkeit
der Gemälde eines Raspal aus mit ihren rohen
Steinmauern, die nur selten getäfelt oder mit Stoff
bespannt, manchmal von Fresken verziert waren: In
ihrem Inneren Laternen, ein Durcheinander von Möbeln aus verschiedenen Generationen, hier und da
gar ein in der Dunkelheit vergessenes Musikzimmer,
Bilder unter dunkelndem Firnis, breite Treppen mit
geschwungenem Schmiedewerk, eine gewisse ab-
weisende Stille, viele Stockflecken, hinter hohen
Mauern Labyrinthe von baumbestandenen Terrassen, überall Palmen. Waren die fünfziger und sechziger Jahre mit ihrem Efeu, den Tuchen aus Jouy und
ihrem Zierat noch von einer gewissen Zurückhal-
tung, einem Rest von Hochmut und Eleganz geprägt,
so rissen die Siebziger und Achtziger die Gebäude
auf, ebneten alles Charakteristische ein, stellten das
Innere aus, übertünchten alles Dunkel-Intime mit
den obligatorischen, pastelligen »Peach«-, »Man-
del«- und »Vanille«-Tönen, machten die Erdge-

snobbery. And it is rich too in the enlightened spirit of painters and writers, native or otherwise, who guard Provence from indignities – sometimes, indeed, inflicted by the Provençaux. In this way the West crossbreeds with the East, tosses off its Indian influences or (via Marseille) those of the rest of the Mediterranean, which, if we are to believe Darius Milhaud, extends from Istanbul to Rio de Janeiro, from *moucharabies* to *azulejos*, taking in the Pompeian atrium on its way. And so a distant vision of this "Arles house" is vouchsafed to me: ideal and paradoxical, composite and coherent, mineral and vegetal, traditional and contemporary, cosmopolitan and local, popular and patrician, astonishing yet reassuring; it is respectful, above all, of the history and geography that compose it, living in osmosis with its inhabitant. This is a land that requires respect, a little acre of mythology over which its myriad subterranean deities mount guard.

The houses which follow as if part of a dream village (for Palladio the town is simply a large house and the house a small town) are, each and every one of them, aspects of a very real dream. Formed as each of them were by Provence – that same Provence that moulded my vision of fashion as surfing on the undulations of a landscape perpetually changing through time – the owners have each created their own Provence. The changes within a house, too, should leave it continuous with its former self. "When the dwelling is finished, there Death enters," says the Arab proverb. So let our labours be ever unfinished.

d'une propriété «dans son jus», imprégnée de la culture «artiste» des Britanniques qui l'avaient respectée bien plus que les notables autochtones qui leur succédèrent. Les beaux jardins en Provence sont presque toujours anglo-saxons. Vieille tradition; le Comtat comme antichambre de la Toscane. C'est que la Provence, comme l'Angleterre ou l'Italie, a la noblesse véritable, primitive, celle de la terre, où la campagne compte plus que la ville, civilisation agreste, poète et paysanne, loin des salons, au-delà des snobismes parisianistes ou bovarystes. Et aussi l'esprit éclairé des peintres ou des écrivains de là ou d'ailleurs, garde-fous et garants de la Provence malgré, parfois, les Provençaux. Ainsi l'Occident métisse l'Orient et balance l'influence des Indes ou, via Marseille, du reste de la Méditerranée, qui va, selon Darius Milhaud, d'Istanbul à Rio de Janeiro, des moucharabiehs aux azulejos en passant par l'atrium pompéien. Je commence à l'entrevoir cette «maison-Arlésienne» idéale et paradoxale, composite et cohérente, minérale et végétale, traditionelle et contemporaine, cosmopolite et locale, populaire et patricienne, étonnante et rassurante, respectueuse, surtout de son histoire et de sa géographie qui la dictent, en osmose avec qui l'habite. C'est une terre qui exige le respect, un arpent de mythologie plein de petits dieux souterrains qui veillent.

Toutes les maisons qui vont suivre dans ce livre comme pour former un village de rêve (pour Palladio la ville n'est rien d'autre qu'une grande maison et la maison n'est rien d'autre qu'une petite ville) toutes ces maisons, donc, sont les facettes d'un mirage bien réel. Chaque propriétaire donne sa version de la Provence mais c'est la Provence qui les a eux-mêmes façonnés comme elle a façonné ma vision de la mode surfant sans cesse sur la vague d'un paysage en perpétuelle évolution. Une maison se doit d'être de même, ni tout à fait la même ni tout à fait une autre. «Quand la demeure est finie la Mort entre», dit un proverbe arabe. Ne la finissons donc jamais!

schosse zu Aquarien, die nach hinten gelegenen, »Souillardes« genannten Küchen zu »Lofts«, »Kitchenettes«, »Bistros«, sie verschandelten alles ringsum aus Ignoranz, Gewinnstreben oder halbverdautem Modernismus.

Ich bin nicht krankhaft in alles Vergangene verliebt. Zeitgenössische Architektur kann mich begeistern, wenn Talent in ihr erkennbar ist. Schließlich ist das Risiko, zusammen mit der Erinnerung die eigene Seele zu verlieren, ebenso groß wie die Gefahr, sich auf einen sterilen lokalen Traditionalismus zurückzuziehen. Als ich 1987 meine Maison de Couture gründete, versuchte ich behutsam, einen verwunschenen Garten mit der Musik der Gypsy Kings und dem Rhythmus des spanischen Nachtlebens in Einklang zu bringen. Seitdem versuche ich mich gemeinsam mit anderen in einem Dasein als Zauberlehrling der so mitreißenden wie schnell vergänglichen Mode – ohne Anmaßung oder Dünkel, so will ich hoffen. Ich hatte an meinen Sohlen etwas von der Provence bis nach Paris mitgebracht und in umgekehrter Richtung etwas Pariserisches in das Land meiner Geburt getragen – zu meiner Überraschung, denn ich hatte eine Zeitlang vergessen, daß die Herkunft sich aus eigener Kraft geltend macht und ich selber, von dieser kraftvollen Welle getragen, weniger »Agent provocateur« war als vielmehr ein Instrument. Also habe ich den Rückzug angetreten. Mein Haus im Süden ist ein Hotel in Arles (das »Hôtel du Nord«!). Und meine Träume erfüllen sich mir in doppelter Weise abseits, der Traum von der Provence westlich im Languedoc und der von der Camargue in der »Kleinen Camargue« westlich von Les Saintes-Maries-de-la-Mer am Fuße der Cevennen, aus denen mein Vater stammt. Und was ist dann Paris für mich? Ein Elfenbeinturm? Nein, ein Observatorium, aus dem ich den Blick auf das Jahr 2000 richte, dazu auf das Rhônetal und einige zusätzliche Schlaglichter: Ein »Schloß meiner Mutter« – einer der Romane von Marcel Pagnol –, ein opal schimmerndes Schlößchen in einem zugleich bäuerlichen und an das Second Empire erinnernden Stil neben der Mühle in Fontvieille, wo Alphonse Daudet seine »Briefe aus meiner Mühle« geschrieben hat, und die Interieurs des Malers und Bühnenbildners

Christian Bérard, eine Hütte auf Pfeilern und eine andere auf einem Baum in Aigues-Mortes, Wohnungen aus dem 16. Jahrhundert in Les-Baux-de-Provence mit terrassenartig angelegten Gärten, Café-Restaurants voll naiver Gemälde, ein Blick auf die »Art Brut« der bedrohten Gebäude am Strand von Beauduc, auf die palladianische Villa in Lambesc, in der eine Amerikanerin ganz nach dem Vorbild des 18. Jahrhunderts lebt, auch, was Essen und Kleidung anbelangt, und Residenzen, die einem Film von Jacques Tati zu entstammen scheinen. Ich erinnere mich auch an ein Anwesen »von altem Schrot und Korn«, geprägt von der künstlerischen Kultur der Briten, die ihr Domizil weit mehr respektiert hatten als die ortsansässigen Notabeln, welche auf sie gefolgt waren. Die schönen Gärten der Provence sind fast alle angelsächsischen Ursprungs. Eine alte Tradition: Das Comtat Venaissin, jene fruchtbare Ebene im Dreieck zwischen der Rhône und dem Fluß Durance, als Vorzimmer der Toskana. In der Provence nämlich lebt wie in England oder Italien ein echter, ursprünglicher, erdnaher Adel, für den das Land mehr zählt als die Stadt; eine im guten Sinne bäuerliche, eine ländlich-poetische Zivilisation fern der Salons, unberührt von allem Großstadt-Snobismus. Überdies kommt ihr der wache Geist der Maler und Schriftsteller zugute; ob diese nun hier geboren sind oder von anderen Orten kommen, sie sind die Irrenwärter und Bürgen der Provence, die sie manchmal sogar vor den Provenzalen schützen müssen. So vermischt sich der Okzident mit dem Orient und verdrängt den Einfluß Indiens oder via Marseille den des restlichen Mittelmeerraums, der, wenn man dem Komponisten Darius Milhaud glauben darf, von Istanbul bis nach Rio de Janeiro reicht, von den byzantinischen Muscharabijes, den Holzgittern vor den Fenstern, über die pompejanischen Atrien bis zu den schmuckvollen Azulejo-Kacheln.

Langsam bildet sich in mir eine Vorstellung von jenem idealen und paradoxen Haus, dem Ziel meiner Träume: Es wird zusammengewürfelt und homogen sein, mineralisch und vegetabil, so traditionell wie zeitgenössisch, so volkstümlich wie herrschaftlich, es sollte Überraschung ebenso vermitteln wie Geborgenheit, soll vor allem die Geschichte und die Geographie respektieren, die es ebenso wie seine Bewohner beeinflussen. Die Provence ist ein Land, das respektiert werden will, ein mythischer Garten voll kleiner unterirdischer Schutzgottheiten.

Alle Häuser, die in diesem Buch gezeigt werden, als sollten sie gemeinsam ein Traumdorf bilden (für Palladio ist übrigens die Stadt nichts anderes als ein großes Haus und ein großes Haus nichts als eine kleine Stadt), all diese Häuser sind Teile eines sehr realen Wunschbildes. Jeder ihrer Eigentümer formuliert sein Bild von der Provence, doch die Provence selber hat jeden einzelnen von ihnen geprägt, wie sie meine Vision von der Mode geprägt hat als etwas, das unaufhörlich auf der Welle einer sich ewig wandelnden Landschaft surft. Mit einem Haus muß es ebenso gehen, weder darf es stets unverändert bleiben noch sich von Grund auf ändern. »Wenn das Haus fertig ist, tritt der Tod ein«, sagt ein arabisches Sprichwort. Lassen wir also immer noch etwas zu tun übrig!

Introduction/Einleitung

de / by / von Lisa Lovatt-Smith
Photos: Edouard Boubat / TOP

> **"Provence has a thousand faces, a thousand aspects, a thousand characters, and it is wrong to describe it as a single and indivisible phenomenon."**
>
> *Jean Giono*

This may seem a rather dry quote from one of Provence's most celebrated writers, who was as severe as the mountain landscape of the Haute-Provence where he was born. Seen through the prism of contemporary sentimentalism that today determines all reference to the region, voices such as Giono's or even Colette's, who echoed him in bantering "Of course you love Provence – but which Provence?", have been submerged by a single assumption in the spirit of Ford Madox Ford, who described Provence as "paradise on Earth". Fuelled by Peter Mayle's sugary best sellers, enthusiasm for the pastoral delights of the area has now reached a fever pitch. From the Carmargue on the Mediterranean, to Barcelonette in the Alpes-Maritimes, Provence is often perceived as a "single and indivisible phenomenon", a bucolic land of lavender fields and fortified hilltop villages. How Giono would have disapproved!

"Provence" is a purely intellectual, or rather emotional, concept. Its borders have long been disputed, not least by the Provençaux themselves. Occupying all the south-eastern corner of France, the "official" Provence comprises five administrative districts or *départements* which together stretch from the Rhône to the Alps. It includes not only the coast where Colette lived, but also the austere highlands celebrated by Giono. The 1904 Nobel Prize winner Frédéric Mistral, the poet who was instrumental in reviving the lost Provençal tongue and who attracted international attention to his cause, defined it thus: "It was the Rhône that made Provence in concert with the wind. Right bank, left bank, kingdom, empire, all are Provence. Of course, its borders are drawn by the language but also by the prevailing wind: the mistral. Wherever the mistral rules, you are in Provence." This other mistral is none other than the infamous wind with which the poet shared his name and which Stendhal described as "Le grand *drawback* de Provence". It does not blow on the Riviera and so excludes this celebrated coastline

«La Provence présente mille visages, mille facettes, mille personnalités et il est vain de la décrire comme un phénomène unique et indivisible.»

Jean Giono

»Die Provence hat tausend Gesichter, tausend Aspekte, tausend Charaktere, und es ist falsch, sie als ein einziges, unteilbares Phänomen darzustellen.«

Jean Giono

Voilà une affirmation quelque peu lapidaire de la part de l'un des écrivains les plus célèbres de Provence... aussi sévère que les paysages montagneux de sa Haute-Provence natale. Devant le sentimentalisme qui affleure aujourd'hui dans la moindre allusion à cette région, des voix telles que celles de Giono ou même de Colette, (qui renchérit sur un ton badin: «Bien sûr que tu aimes la Provence, mais quelle Provence?») sont étouffées par celles qui décrivent la Provence comme un paradis terrestre. Alimenté par les best-sellers de l'anglais Peter Mayle, l'engouement pour la région bat aujourd'hui son plein. De la Camargue à la Méditerranée, de Barcelonette aux Alpes-Maritimes, la Provence est souvent perçue comme un «phénomène unique et indivisible», une terre bucolique de champs de lavande et de villages fortifiés perchés à la cime des collines. Giono doit se retourner dans sa tombe!

La «Provence» est un concept purement intellectuel, ou disons plutôt, purement affectif. Ses frontières sont disputées depuis toujours, et pas seulement par les Provençaux. Occupant le Sud-Est de la France, la Provence «officielle» s'étend du Rhône aux Alpes. Elle comprend la Côte d'Azur où Colette a vécu, mais aussi les hauteurs austères célébrées par Giono. Frédéric Mistral, lauréat du prix Nobel en 1904, a fortement contribué à la renaissance de la langue provençale et à attirer l'attention du monde entier sur sa cause: «Mais c'est le Rhône qui a fait la Provence, d'accord avec le vent. Rive droite, rive gauche, royaume, empire, tout cela c'est la Provence. Elle est délimitée encore, bien entendu, par la langue, mais aussi par le vent maître: le mistral. Partout où il règne, vous êtes en Provence.» Ce redoutable vent auquel le poète doit son nom n'avait pas les faveurs de Stendhal, qui le qualifiait de «grand inconvénient de la Provence». Il ne sévit pas sur la Côte d'Azur, ce qui exclut le célèbre littoral de la définition de Mistral. D'ailleurs, la différence est notable: l'esthétique de la Côte d'Azur est le fruit

Dieser Satz aus der Feder eines der berühmtesten provenzalischen Schriftsteller mag recht trocken klingen, ebenso streng wie die Berglandschaft der Haute-Provence, wo er geboren wurde. Wenn man die Dinge nur im Licht der sentimentalen Attitüde sieht, die die meisten derzeitigen Äußerungen über diese Region prägt, werden Stimmen wie die Gionos oder Colettes, die mit ihrer scherzhaften Frage: »Natürlich lieben Sie die Provence – nur welche Provence?«, den gleichen Standpunkt vertrat, durch ein einziges pauschales Urteil wie das von Ford Madox Ford vom Tisch gewischt; dieser nämlich nannte die Provence das »Paradies auf Erden«. Bestärkt durch Peter Mayles süßliche Bestseller hat die Begeisterung für bukolische Genüsse mittlerweile den Siedepunkt erreicht. Die Provence, von der Camargue am Mittelmeer bis Barcelonette in den Alpes-Maritimes, wird oft als »ein einziges, unteilbares Phänomen«, als Land der Hirten, der Lavendelfelder und befestigten Bergdörfer begriffen.

Die »Provence« existiert lediglich als rein intellektuelle oder eher noch als emotionale Vorstellung. Ihre tatsächlichen Grenzen sind seit langem umstritten, nicht zuletzt bei den *provençaux* selbst. Die »offizielle« Provence in der südöstlichen Ecke Frankreichs umfaßt fünf Verwaltungsbezirke oder Départements, die sich von der Rhône bis zu den Alpen erstrecken. Dazu gehört nicht nur die Küste, an der Colette lebte, sondern auch das von Giono so gepriesene, karge Hochland. Frédéric Mistral, Dichter und Nobelpreisträger von 1904, der maßgeblich an der Wiederbelebung der fast verlorenen provenzalischen Sprache beteiligt war und die Aufmerksamkeit der internationalen Öffentlichkeit auf sein Anliegen richtete, meinte: »Doch es war die Rhône, die der Provence ihr Gesicht gab, zusammen mit dem Wind. Rechtes Ufer, linkes Ufer, Königreich, Kaiserreich, all das ist die Provence. Natürlich sind ihre Grenzen bis heute auch durch die Sprache gekennzeichnet, vor allem aber durch den vorherr-

from Mistral's definition. The aesthetics of the Côte d'Azur are the fruit of five centuries of Italian occupation, and above all else it is the influence of the Mediterranean that dominates the lifestyle and the cuisine there.

The mistral does, however, blow in the Roman town of Nîmes, now part of the *département* of the Gard and no longer "officially" Provence. What is more, Nîmes was the birthplace of Mistral's great friend, Alphonse Daudet, who could not possibly be considered as anything less than a Provençal writer! Mistral's

> "Empire of delight and exhilaration,
> Imaginary Empire of Provence
> Mere mention of your name enchants the world!"

thus included the western bank of the river Rhône, historically a great barrier.

Ford Madox Ford called Provence "a highway along which travelled continually the stream of the arts, of thought, of the traditions of life". Although united and part of France since the end of the 15th century it has remained decentralized and inimitable, a sum of all its different parts. Life in Provence reflects the imperatives of rural existence and is thus closely linked to the diversity of its landscape. Giono estimated that in a day's travelling across the region one would come across as many as five hundred different landscapes – and ways of living.

For Jean Giono, born in Manosque in 1895, the solitary life of the shepherds, migrating with the seasons, or of the villagers from the highlands near Forcalquier and Sisteron embodied the true expression of Provence. Their reality was far removed from the cardboard image of nature at its most Arcadian that other writers have evoked. It must be said, however, that in his own way Giono had an equally romanticized vision of rustic existence: something along the lines of the Puritan ideal of redemption through toil, struggle, silence and abstinence. His was perhaps a literary reaction to the ravages of the industrial age and a presentiment of what was to come. His entire *œuvre* is a moving homage to the Haute-Provence. "The highlands are disconcerting... The violence of this part of Provence has held neigh-

de cinq siècles d'occupation italienne, et c'est avant tout l'influence de la Méditerranée qui domine dans son art de vivre et sa cuisine.

En revanche, le mistral souffle sur la ville romaine de Nîmes, désormais rattachée au département du Gard et non plus à la Provence «officielle». En outre, Nîmes est la ville natale du grand ami de Mistral, Alphonse Daudet, que l'on peut difficilement considérer autrement que comme un grand auteur provençal!
La Provence de Mistral,

«Empire de plaisance et d'allégresse,
Empire fantastique de Provence
Qui avec ton nom seul charme le monde!»
s'étend donc outre le Rhône, depuis toujours grande ligne de partage, et inclut sa rive ouest.

Ford Madox Ford a défini la Provence comme «une grande route empruntée de tous temps par le courant des arts, de la pensée et des traditions». Bien qu'intégrée à la France depuis la fin du XVe siècle, elle a gardé son individualité. La vie provençale reflète les impératifs du monde rural et elle est donc étroitement liée à la diversité de son relief. Giono estimait qu'en traversant la région en une journée, on rencontrait près de cinq cents types de paysages différents ... et autant de façons de vivre.

Pour Jean Giono, né à Manosque en 1895, l'existence solitaire des bergers transhumants ou des habitants des villages haut perchés de Forcalquier et de Sisteron était la véritable expression de la Provence. Leur réalité est bien loin de l'image d'Epinal évoquée par d'autres écrivains. Cela dit, la vision de Giono n'est pas dénuée d'un certain romantisme: elle est imprégnée d'une sorte d'idéal puritain de la rédemption par le dur labeur, le combat quotidien pour la survie, le silence et l'abstinence. Sans doute était-ce une réaction littéraire aux ravages de l'ère industrielle, un pressentiment des bouleversements à venir. Son œuvre toute entière est un vibrant hommage à la Haute-Provence: «Les hautes terres déroutent ... La violence de cet endroit de Provence en a écarté les voisins et les caravanes. Il a gardé sa pureté préhistorique et c'est elle qui brusquement vous pousse sur des nouveaux chemins. On n'est jamais venu regarder la Provence

schenden Wind: den Mistral. Überall dort, wo er weht, befinden Sie sich in der Provence.« Dieser andere Mistral, mit dem der Dichter den Namen teilte, ist jener fürchterliche Wind, den Stendhal »le grand *drawback*« – den großen Nachteil – der Provence nannte. An der Riviera weht er nicht, damit ist die vielgepriesene Küste nach Mistrals Definition ausgeschlossen. Es gibt tatsächlich Unterschiede, denn die Schönheiten der Côte d'Azur sind das Erbe einer fünf Jahrhunderte dauernden italienischen Besatzungszeit: hier prägt der Mittelmeerraum Lebensart und Küche.

Der Mistral weht allerdings in der römischen Stadt Nîmes, die heute zum Département du Gard gehört und damit nicht mehr zur »offiziellen« Provence. Außerdem wurde in Nîmes Mistrals bester Freund Alphonse Daudet geboren, ein provenzalischer Schriftsteller *par excellence*. Mistrals Zeilen

»Reich der Freuden und der Fröhlichkeit,
Phantastisches Reich der Provence,
Schon dein Name bezaubert die Welt!«
schlossen insofern das Westufer der Rhône mit ein, die historisch immer die Trennlinie gebildet hat.

Ford Madox Ford nannte die Provence eine »Autobahn, auf der ein kontinuierlicher Strom von Kunstwerken, Gedanken und Traditionen reiste«. Auch nach der Vereinigung und Eingliederung ins französische Reich im 15. Jahrhundert widersetzte sich die Provence der Zentralisierung und blieb unverwechselbar, die Summe ihrer Einzelteile. Das Leben in der Provence spiegelt die Zwänge des bäuerlichen Daseins und ist deshalb eng mit der jeweiligen Landschaft verknüpft. Giono meinte, bei einer Tagesreise durch die Region begegne man wohl bis zu fünfhundert verschiedenen Landschaften – und Lebensweisen.

Für Jean Giono, der 1895 in Manosque geboren wurde, war das einsame Leben der Hirten auf den Sommerweiden oder der Dörfler im Hochland nahe Forcalquier und Sisteron der wahre Inbegriff der Provence. Ihre Realität ist weit entfernt von dem kitschigen Bild einer arkadischen Natur, das andere Autoren malten. Man muß allerdings zugeben, daß Giono selbst eine nicht minder romantische Sicht des bäuerlichen Lebens vertrat, die sich vage am

bours and convoys at a distance. It has preserved its historic purity and it abruptly pushes you along new paths. No one ever came to look at Provence from here. And yet it is from here that it flows all around, from this bare ground."

The highland, thus evoked, borders with the *département* of the Var at the Gorges du Verdon, one of the most sumptuous natural landscapes in France. The Var is home to the over-stretched charms of Saint-Tropez, and its fertile hinterland that had so pleased Victor Hugo: "The plain is delightful, it is so green and shady. Each of these trees does something for man; they are useful as well as attractive. The olive tree gives its fruit, the orange tree its blossom, the mulberry tree its leaf, the cork oak its bark, the pine its sap."

The adjacent mountain territory of the Lubéron had its very own bard in the writer Henri Bosco long before the contemporary invasion by artists and weekenders. On this subject it is interesting to note that, in a guide to Provence published as recently as 1969, the Lubéron was still described as "uninhabited" and "inpenetrable".

Bosco's mid-century appreciation of the mountain was essentially spiritual and is perceived as a reaction to rationalism. He was to celebrate the Lubéron in most of his work. Brought up on the Avignon plain, he longed for the highlands, and was fascinated by the discovery of the ambiguity of the mountain range – verdant and generous on one face, wild on the other. It was a land that "... *knows*, a landscape that reflects the deep truths of life ..." Later, Maurice Barrès was also to write feelingly of the region: "Poor soil, which yields sparse crops, a few almonds, a few truffles, a forest whose sparseness would make someone from the North smile; but it is in this wilderness that the divine grace of Provence can be felt."

The craggy little mountains known as the Alpilles close to the lowlands of the mouth of the Rhône are studded with exceptional Provençal towns: Avignon, Aix, Arles, Marseille, all of which bear the imprint of Caesar's colonization of the first Roman *provincia*. They are all very different from each other: Avignon is a walled papal city. Unmistak-

d'ici. C'est pourtant d'ici qu'elle coule tout autour à partir de cet émergement nu.»

Les hautes terres ainsi évoquées confinent, avec le département du Var, aux Gorges du Verdon, l'un des paysages les plus spectaculaires de France. Le Var offre les charmes surexploités de Saint-Tropez et de son arrière-pays luxuriant qui plaisait tant à Victor Hugo: «La plaine est ravissante tant elle est verte et ombragée. Tous ces arbres-là font quelque chose pour l'homme: ils sont utiles en même temps que charmants. L'olivier donne son fruit, l'oranger sa fleur, le mûrier sa feuille, le chêne-liège son écorce, le pin sa sève.»

Bien avant d'être envahi par les artistes et les résidences secondaires, le massif adjacent du Lubéron possédait lui aussi son barde en la personne d'Henri Bosco. D'ailleurs, un guide de Provence publié en 1969 décrit encore le Lubéron comme «inhabité» et «impénétrable». Vers le milieu de ce siècle, Bosco prêtait à la montagne une dimension spirituelle, ce que l'on interpréta comme une réaction au rationalisme. Ayant grandi dans la plaine d'Avignon, il rêvait des hauteurs et était fasciné par le caractère ambigu de cette chaîne de montagnes dont un versant était généreux et l'autre, sauvage. La plupart de ses œuvres célèbrent cette terre qui «sait, ce paysage qui reflète les vérités profondes de la vie». Plus tard, Maurice Barrès dirait de la région: «Pauvre terrain, qui n'a que des produits rares, quelque amandes, quelques truffes, une forêt dont la maigreur ferait sourire un homme du Nord; mais c'est tout à l'abandon, la grâce divine de la Provence.»

Les petites montagnes escarpées des Alpilles qui jouxtent les terres basses des Bouches-du-Rhône, sont parsemées de villes provençales exceptionnelles: Avignon, Aix, Arles, Marseille, toutes portant encore l'empreinte de la colonisation par César de la première «provincia» romaine. Elles sont très différentes les unes des autres: Avignon est une ville papale fortifiée, résolument méridionale, que Stendhal comparait à une ville italienne, Mérimée à l'Espagne et Victor Hugo à Athènes. Pour le voyageur qui descend du nord, elle offre un avant-goût du Midi. Avec sa gare et son aéroport qui en font au-

puritanischen Ideal der Erlösung durch Mühsal, Kampf, Schweigen und Abstinenz orientierte. Vielleicht war dies eine literarische Reaktion auf die Verwüstungen durch das Industriezeitalter, eine Vorahnung dessen, was noch kommen sollte. Sein gesamtes Werk ist eine bewegende Hommage an die Haute-Provence: »Das Hochland schreckt ab... Das Rauhe dieses Teiles der Provence hält Nachbarn und Karawanen fern. Es hat seine prähistorische Reinheit bewahrt, und von dieser wird man unversehens auf neue Wege gestoßen. Niemand ist je hergekommen, um sich die Provence von hier aus anzusehen. Und dennoch fließt sie von hier aus überall hin, ausgehend von diesem nackten ersten Erscheinen.«

Das so charakterisierte Hochland grenzt bei den Gorges du Verdon, einer der großartigsten Naturlandschaften Frankreichs, an das Département Var. Das Var seinerseits beherbergt die überspannten Attraktionen von Saint-Tropez, aber auch ein fruchtbares Hinterland, das Victor Hugo so gut gefiel: »Die Ebene ist herrlich, so überaus grün und schattig. Jeder dieser Bäume tut etwas für den Menschen; sie sind ebenso nützlich wie schön anzusehen. Der Ölbaum schenkt uns seine Früchte, der Orangenbaum seine Blüten, der Maulbeerbaum seine Blätter, die Korkeiche ihre Rinde und die Kiefer ihr Harz.«

Das angrenzende Berggebiet des Lubéron hatte seinen eigenen Barden in dem Schriftsteller Henri Bosco, lange bevor moderne Künstler und Wochenendgäste hier einfielen. Interessanterweise wurde der Lubéron in einem erst 1969 veröffentlichten Reiseführer noch als »unbewohnt« und »unzugänglich« beschrieben. Boscos Liebe zu diesem Gebirge Mitte dieses Jahrhunderts war überwiegend spiritueller Natur und wird als Reaktion auf den vorherrschenden Rationalismus verstanden. Der in der Ebene von Avignon aufgewachsene Bosco sehnte sich nach den Bergen und war fasziniert von ihrem Widerspruch, ihrer üppig grünen, großzügigen, zugleich aber wilden Erscheinung. Er pries den Lubéron in den meisten seiner Werke. Es ist ein Land, das »... *weiß*, eine Landschaft, die die tiefen Wahrheiten des Lebens spiegelt...« Später schrieb auch Maurice Barrès einfühlsam über diese Region:

ably southern, it was compared by Stendhal to an Italian town, by Prosper Mérimée to Spain and by Victor Hugo to Athens. It offers the first taste of "Le Midi" for the traveller who comes from the north. A large, bustling market town with a train station and airport that nowadays are the real gateways to Provence, it has retained its power to surprise. Mérimée, upon arrival remarked: "The language, the costumes, the appearance of the country all seemed strange to someone coming from the centre of France." Aix-en-Provence is something else again – as civilized and gracious as her splendidly restrained 18th-century architecture. Marseille, that Stendhal, when travelling in the early 19th century, liked very much and called the "ville du Midi par excellence", is the official capital of Provence. It is now a bustling international port swollen with progressive waves of immigration. Roman Arles belongs spiritually to Spain, with its corridas and animated street life. Daudet went so far as to portray the perfume of a certain Orientalism in its narrow medina-like streets, "this marvellous little town, one of the most picturesque in France, with its sculpted, rounded balconies, looking like pierced Arab screens overhanging into the middle of the narrow streets, with old, blackened houses whose small Moorish doors are low and pointed."

Daudet was then to travel on to the Camargue, the salty marshlands now home to a vast nature reserve for pink flamingos, wild horses and bulls. It is here that every year gypsies from all over Europe gather to render homage to their patron saint, Sara. The writer described its melancholy charms: "As far as the eye can see, among the pastures and marshes, rose madder glints among the saltwort. Bunches of tamarisk and reeds stand like islands in a calm sea. No tall trees. The flat, immense expanse of the plain is undisturbed. In the distance a few folds extend their low roofs almost to ground level. Scattered flocks of sheep, lying in the saline grasses or wandering together around the russet cape of the shepherd do nothing to interrupt the great uniform line, reduced as they are by this infinite expanse of blue horizons and open sky. As if from a huge sea, despite its waves, a feeling of soli-

jourd'hui la véritable porte de la Provence, ce grand bourg a conservé sa capacité à surprendre. S'y rendant pour la première fois, Prosper Mérimée observa: «La langue, les costumes, l'aspect même du pays, tout dépayse pour celui qui arrive du centre de la France.» Aix-en-Provence est encore un autre univers: aussi civilisée et élégante que son architecture du XVIIIe siècle. Marseille, très appréciée de Stendhal qui, au début du XIXe siècle, l'appelait «la ville du Midi par excellence», est la capitale officielle de la Provence. C'est désormais un grand port international aux limites sans cesse repoussées par les vagues successives d'immigration. Avec ses «corridas» et ses rues animées, Arles la Romaine appartient spirituellement à l'Espagne. Daudet a évoqué le parfum d'un certain orientalisme dans le dédale de ses ruelles qui rappelle la médina: «Cette merveilleuse petite ville, une des plus pittoresques de France avec ses balcons sculptés, arrondis, s'avançant comme des moucharabiehs jusqu'au milieu des rues étroites, avec ses vieilles maisons noires aux petites portes mauresques, ogivales et basses.»

Daudet devait ensuite se rendre en Camargue, terre de marais salants qui accueille désormais un vaste parc naturel où abondent flamants roses et troupeaux sauvages de chevaux et de taureaux. Ici, les Gitans venus des quatre coins d'Europe se rassemblent chaque année pour rendre hommage à sainte Sara, leur patronne. Daudet fut séduit par le charme de cette terre: «A perte de vue, parmi les pâturages, des marais, des roubines luisent dans les salicornes. Des bouquets de tamaris et des roseaux font des îlots comme sur une mer calme. Pas d'arbres hauts. L'aspect uni, immense, de la plaine n'est pas troublé. De loin en loin, des parcs de bestiaux étendent leurs toits bas presque au ras de terre. Des troupeaux dispersés, couchés dans les herbes salines, ou cheminant serrés autour de la cape rousse du berger, n'interrompent pas la grande ligne uniforme amoindris qu'ils sont par cet espace infini d'horizons bleus et de ciel ouvert. Comme de la mer unie malgré ses vagues, il se dégage de cette plaine un sentiment de solitude, d'immensité, accru encore par le mistral qui souffle sans relâche, sans

»Schlechter Boden, der nur magere Erträge liefert, ein paar Mandeln, ein paar Trüffeln, ein Wald, der so licht ist, daß jemand aus dem Norden darüber lächeln würde; doch alles ist Wildnis, der himmlische Charme der Provence.«

Das zerklüftete kleine Gebirge der Alpilles nahe dem Flachland der Rhône-Mündung ist ringsum von bedeutenden provenzalischen Städten umgeben: Avignon, Aix, Arles, Marseille, allesamt geprägt von Cäsars Kolonisierung der ersten römischen *provincia*. Sie sind völlig unterschiedlich: Avignon ist eine von hohen Mauern umgebene Papststadt mit unverkennbar südlichem Flair. Stendhal verglich sie mit italienischen Städten, Prosper Mérimée mit Spanien und Victor Hugo mit Athen. Sie ist der erste Vorgeschmack auf »Le Midi« für denjenigen, der von Norden anreist. Die große, geschäftige Marktstadt mit ihrem Bahnhof und Flughafen, die heutzutage die Tore zur Provence bilden, ist trotzdem noch immer für Überraschungen gut. Aix-en-Provence wiederum ist ganz anders, ebenso kultiviert und anmutig wie seine prachtvolle und doch zurückhaltende Architektur aus dem 18. Jahrhundert. Marseille, das Stendhal bei seinem Aufenthalt Anfang des 19. Jahrhundert sehr schätzte und das er als die »südfranzösische Stadt *par excellence*« bezeichnete, ist die offizielle Hauptstadt der Provence und heute eine quirlige internationale Hafenstadt, deren Bevölkerung sich durch mehrere Einwanderungswellen stark vermehrt hat. Das römische Arles mit seinen Corridas und dem regen Straßenleben gehört innerlich im Grunde zu Spanien. Daudet ging sogar soweit, den engen Gassen der an eine Medina erinnernden Altstadt eine gewisse orientalischen Note zuzuschreiben: »Diese wunderschöne kleine Stadt, eine der malerischsten Frankreichs mit ihren geschnitzten, abgerundeten Balkonen, die wie durchbrochene arabische Erker mitten über der schmalen Straße hängen, mit alten, geschwärzten Häusern und ihren winzigen maurischen Türen, die niedrig und mit Spitzbögen versehen sind.«

Daudet reiste von hier aus weiter in die salzige Sumpflandschaft der Camargue, die heute ein riesiges Naturschutzgebiet für rosa Flamingos, wilde Pferde und Stiere ist. Hier versammeln sich jedes

tude, of immensity emanates from this plain, rein-
forced by the mistral which blows relentlessly, unhin-
dered, and whose powerful gusts seem to flatten
and widen the landscape. Everything bows before it.
The merest bushes retain the imprint of its passage,
remaining twisted, hunched southwards in an
attitude of perpetual flight."

These then are the multiple facets of Provence, a land that exists in the imagination rather
than on the maps. In the words of Lawrence Durell:
"It is not really a separate entity with boundaries and
a separated, self-realized soul as, say, Switzerland is.
It is a beautiful metaphor born of Caesar's impatience with a geographical corridor stacked with the
ruins of a hundred cultures, a hundred nations and
tribes, a hundred armies... From the purely historical
point of view, what seems remarkable is the long
tally of violence and drama which characterizes this
land of green glades and noble forests, a minor
paradise if ever there was one. Yet Goths, Franks,
Vandals, Saracens, every variety of invader seems
to have subjected it to the extremes of pillage, destruction, naked war. It was as if its beauty was
too much for them, they went berserk."

Today's tourists, one might ironize, are set to
do the same. In much the same way that the Côte
d'Azur became an international playground in the
thirties, when resorts replaced fishing villages, the
phenomenon is repeating itself in the Lubéron and
the Alpilles. Ring roads and roundabouts, built to
deal with tourist traffic, have replaced vineyards and
farmland. More importantly, the growth of the su-
perstore has provoked the gradual erosion of village
life that had traditionally been centred around the
boulangerie, *boucherie* and *épicerie*. Hilltop villages
such as Lacoste, Roussillon and Ménerbes have become luxury colonies; houses restored by Parisians
and foreigners have replaced working people's
homes. Such is the price of popularity. And yet without it, rural depopulation, the bastard child of the industrial age, would have perhaps succeeded in re-
ducing to desolation a mythical land famed and
fought over since the Greeks.

Provence Interiors   Introduction de Lisa Lovatt-Smith

obstacle, et qui, de son haleine puissante, semble aplanir, agrandir le paysage. Tout se courbe devant lui. Les moindres arbustes gardent l'empreinte de son passage, en restent tordus, couchés vers le sud dans l'attitude d'une fuite perpétuelle.»

Telles sont donc les multiples facettes de la Provence, une terre qui existe dans l'imagination plutôt que sur les cartes. Selon les termes de Lawrence Durell: «Il ne s'agit pas vraiment d'une entité à part, avec des frontières et une âme autonome comme, disons, la Suisse. C'est une belle métaphore née de l'impatience de César devant un couloir géographique encombré des ruines de cent cultures, de cent nations et tribus, de cent armées... D'un point de vue purement historique, on est frappé par le long enchaînement de tragédies et de violences qui se sont abattues sur cette terre de clairières vertes et de nobles forêts, un véritable petit paradis s'il y en eu jamais un. Goths, Francs, Vandales, Sarrasins, et toutes autres espèces d'envahisseurs se sont acharnés à lui infliger les extrêmes du pillage, de la destruction et de la guerre la plus brutale. Comme si devant tant de beauté, ils en avaient perdu la raison.»

On pourrait dire, ironiquement, que les touristes d'aujourd'hui perpétuent cette tradition. Le Lubéron et les Alpilles subissent peu à peu le même sort que la Côte d'Azur, devenue terre de loisir internationale dans les années trente, quand les stations balnéaires ont peu à peu remplacé les ports de pêche. Les bretelles d'autoroute et les ronds-points, construits pour endiguer le flot des touristes, ont remplacé les vignobles et les fermes. Plus inquiétant encore, l'avènement de la grande surface entraîne l'érosion progressive de la vie de village, traditionnellement regroupée autour des petits commerces comme la boulangerie, l'épicerie et la boucherie. Les villages en nid d'aigle comme Lacoste, Roussillon et Ménerbes sont devenus des colonies de luxe: les maisons restaurées par les Parisiens et les étrangers ont remplacé les humbles demeures des autochtones. Tel est le prix à payer pour la popularité. Pourtant, sans elle, l'exode rural aurait sans doute condamné à la désolation cette terre mythique que l'on célèbre et que l'on s'arrache depuis l'Antiquité.

Jahr Zigeuner aus ganz Europa, um ihre Schutzpatronin Sara zu verehren. Daudet beschrieb den melancholischen Reiz dieser Region: »Soweit das Auge reicht, lugt zwischen den Weiden und Sümpfen Färberkrapp zwischen dem Salzkraut hervor. Tamariskenbüschel und Schilf bilden Inseln wie in einer glatten See. Keine hohen Bäume. Die gleichförmige, immense Wirkung der Ebene wird durch nichts gestört. In der Ferne breiten ein paar Viehpferche ihre niedrigen Dächer fast bis zum Erdboden aus. Wie vom Meer, das seinen Wellen zum Trotz eine Einheit bildet, geht von dieser Ebene ein Gefühl der Einsamkeit, der Unendlichkeit aus, verstärkt noch vom Mistral, der ohne Unterlaß, ohne Hindernis weht und der mit seinem mächtigen Atem die Landschaft flacher, weiter zu machen scheint. Alles beugt sich vor ihm. Noch die kleinsten Sträucher tragen die Male seines Durchzugs, bleiben gekrümmt, nach Süden geneigt wie in einer Haltung immerwährender Flucht.«

Dies also sind die vielfältigen Facetten der Provence, eines Landes, das eher in der Vorstellung als auf den Landkarten existiert. Was sich in den dreißiger Jahren abspielte, als die Côte d'Azur zur Spielwiese der internationalen Schickeria wurde und Fischerdörfer sich in Badeorte verwandelten, wiederholt sich nun im Lubéron und in den Alpilles. Um des mobilen Touristenansturms Herr zu werden, werden Umgehungsstraßen gebaut, wo vorher Weinberge und Äcker waren. Noch einschneidender ist, daß die riesigen Supermärkte das Leben in den kleinen Orten, das sich traditionell rund um *Boulangerie*, *Boucherie* und *Epicerie* abspielt, allmählich zum Erliegen bringt. Bergdörfer wie Lacoste, Roussillon und Ménerbes sind zu luxuriösen Kolonien mutiert, und die von Parisern und Ausländern renovierten Häuser haben die Wohnungen der Arbeiter verdrängt. Dies ist der Preis der Popularität – doch ohne sie wäre es der Landflucht, diesem unerwünschten Abkömmling des Industriezeitalters, womöglich gelungen, das mythische, seit den Griechen berühmte und ersehnte Land zu entvölkern.

Pierre, always known as "Pepe", is something of a notable among the Manouche, the Provençal gypsies. He is the official clan chief, elected year after year to carry the statue of Sara, the patron Saint of the gypsies, on his broad shoulders. Sara is said to have been the dark-skinned handmaiden of Saints Mary Jacobé and Mary Salomé who landed in the Camargue after fleeing Palestine. She is considered the ancestor of all gypsies and celebrated with a mass, a midnight watch and a procession every May in Les Saintes-Maries-de-la-Mer. For the last 40 years Pepe has made his pilgrimage from wherever in Provence he might be sojourning, in his brightly painted wooden caravan which is practically a Provençal landmark. He proudly points out his 13 children and 65 grandchildren, all of whom have spent a considerable amount of their childhood among the chintz and lace of Pepe's interior-on-wheels. Few of them, however, seem disposed to follow in Pepe's footsteps and have long abandoned the traditional wooden caravans.

Pierre Lafleur

Pierre, alias «Pépé», fait figure de notable parmi les manouches. C'est le chef de clan officiel, réélu chaque année pour porter la statue de Sara, sainte patronne des gitans, sur ses larges épaules. On raconte que Sara était la servante à la peau mate des saintes Marie-Jacobé et Marie-Salomé qui débarquèrent en Camargue après avoir fui la Palestine. Considérée comme l'ancêtre de tous les gitans, on célèbre sa mémoire chaque mois de mai lors d'une messe, d'une veillée et d'une procession aux Saintes-Maries-de-la-Mer. Depuis quarante ans, Pépé ne manque jamais ce pèlerinage. Quel que soit le coin de Provence où il se trouve, il arrive au rendez-vous dans sa roulotte bigarrée qui est devenue pratiquement une institution provençale. Il parle fièrement de ses treize enfants et soixante-cinq petits enfants, qui ont tous usé leurs fonds de culotte sur les chintz et les dentelles de la maison roulante de Pépé. Toutefois, la plupart d'entre eux ont abandonné depuis longtemps la roulotte traditionnelle en bois.

Pierre, den alle nur »Pepe« nennen, ist eine Berühmtheit bei den Manouches, den provenzalischen Zigeunern. Er ist der offizielle Sippenchef, und ihm kommt Jahr für Jahr die Ehre zu, die Statue Saras, der Schutzpatronin der Zigeuner, auf seinen starken Schultern zu tragen. Der Legende nach war Sara das dunkelhäutige Dienstmädchen der Heiligen Maria Jakobäa und Maria Salome, die nach ihrer Flucht aus Palästina in der Camargue strandeten. Sie gilt als Ahnmutter aller Zigeuener, und ihr zu Ehren finden jedes Jahr im Mai in Les Saintes-Maries-de-la-Mer eine Nachtwache, eine frühmorgendliche Messe und eine Prozession statt. In den letzten vierzig Jahren hat Pepe, von jedem Ort der Provence aus, an dem er sich gerade aufhielt, die Wallfahrt in seinem bunt bemalten Holzwagen angetreten, der mittlerweile schon so etwas wie ein provenzalisches Wahrzeichen ist. Stolz erzählt er von seinen 13 Kindern und 65 Enkeln, die alle einen beträchtlichen Teil ihrer Kindheit in Pepes mit Chintz und Spitze angefüllter rollender Wohnung verbracht haben. Nur wenige von ihnen scheinen jedoch bereit zu sein, es Pepe nachzutun; die meisten haben seit langem die traditionellen hölzernen Wohnwagen aufgegeben.

The gypsy caravan: This brightly-painted horse-drawn caravan is one of the very few still to be seen in Provence, traditionally an important centre for gypsies. All romantic notions of the Romany way of life, pictured as a rustic existence in a pretty little caravan such as this one, are quickly dispelled during a visit to the gypsy festival at Les Saintes-Maries-de-la-Mer. Modern wanderers, it can quickly be seen, prefer the convenience of motorized caravans. In any event, the widespread tradition of burning the family caravan when one of the couple dies, ensures that few antique caravans remain. Owned by a guitar-playing gypsy nicknamed "Boy", this example, made in Manosque, is in sheet-iron and wood. The tendency, worldwide, is for gypsies to become more stationary and this caravan has recently retired from wandering the roads. Along with the horse that towed it, the caravan has taken up permanent residence on the road from Les Saintes-Maries-de-la-Mer to Aigues-Mortes, the stretch of coast that van Gogh loved to paint.

Une roulotte de gitans

Cette roulotte haute en couleurs est l'un des dernières que l'on puisse voir en Provence, lieu de passage traditionnel des gitans. L'idée romantique qu'on se fait d'une vie bucolique de bohémiens, allant de par les routes dans une jolie petite roulotte telle que celle-ci, est vite dissipée lorsqu'on se rend au pèlerinage gitan des Saintes-Maries-de-la-Mer. Ces voyageurs modernes préfèrent désormais le confort des caravanes motorisées. En outre, la tradition très répandue de brûler la roulotte de famille à la mort d'un des membres du couple, fait que très peu de modèles anciens sont parvenus jusqu'à nous. Celle-ci appartient à «Boy», un guitariste gitan. Construite à Manosque, elle est en tôle et en bois. Dans le monde entier, les gitans tendent à se sédentariser et Boy n'échappe pas à la règle. Avec le cheval qui la tirait, cette roulotte a récemment élu domicile sur la route qui mène des Saintes-Maries-de-la-Mer à Aigues-Mortes, ce segment de route que Van Gogh aimait tant peindre.

Der Zigeunerwagen: Dieser bunt bemalte Pferdewagen ist einer der wenigen, die man heute noch in der Provence zu Gesicht bekommt, wo seit jeher zahlreiche Zigeuner leben. Die romantische Vorstellung vom »lustigen« Zigeunerleben und einem idyllischen Dasein in einem hübschen kleinen Wohnwagen wie diesem löst sich rasch in Luft auf, wenn man das Zigeunerfest in Les Saintes-Maries-de-la-Mer besucht. Moderne Nomaden, das erkennt man recht bald, bevorzugen die Bequemlichkeiten motorisierter Wohnwagen. Zudem sorgt die weit verbreitete Tradition, den Wohnwagen der Familie zu verbrennen, wenn ein Ehepartner stirbt, in jedem Fall dafür, daß nur sehr wenige alte Zigeunerwagen erhalten geblieben sind. Der hier vorgestellte Wagen gehört einem gitarrespielenden Zigeuner mit dem Spitznamen »Boy« und wurde in Manosque aus Weißblech und Holz gebaut. Weltweit neigen Zigeuner heute mehr zur Seßhaftigkeit, und auch dieser Wohnwagen ist seit kurzem nicht mehr auf den Straßen unterwegs. Zusammen mit dem Zugpferd wurde er als fester Wohnsitz an der Straße zwischen Les Saintes-Maries-de-la-Mer und Aigues-Mortes abgestellt, an dem Teil der Küste, den van Gogh gern malte.

This caravan is particularly small, and yet traditionally would have lodged a family of four or five. The inside of the caravan features two dressers for storage, a raised bed and a small wood-burning stove. The lace curtains at the windows are typical of gypsy interiors.

Particulièrement petite, cette roulotte aurait autrefois accueilli une famille de quatre ou cinq personnes. L'intérieur de la roulotte comporte deux commodes pour le rangement, un lit surélevé et un petit poêle à charbon. Les rideaux en dentelle sont typiques des intérieurs gitans.

Der Wohnwagen ist winzig; trotzdem hätte darin früher eine vier- bis fünfköpfige Familie gelebt. Im Innern des Wohnwagens befinden sich zwei Schränke, ein erhöhtes Bett und ein kleiner Holzofen. Die Spitzenvorhänge vor den Fenstern sind typisch für Zigeunerwagen.

This eccentric couple of painters live in a brightly-painted gypsy caravan and a "cabane camarguaise" on a plot of land right by the sea and within view of the church of Les Saintes-Maries-de-la-Mer. Barrera, originally Russian, came to the Camargue by way of an adventurous life that included a few name changes, many narrow escapes, a wartime spell in the Secret Service, another in a Marseille prison and, finally, a desire for a quieter life far from the city streets. Inken Drozd arrived at the door of the "cabane" one day, during one of Barrera's celebrated gypsy parties, and stayed. Together they have a philosophical and generous outlook on life, welcoming friends to tea in the caravan or for an early aperitif whilst gazing upon the pink flamingos that populate the lagoon at sunset.

Nicolas Barrera et Inken Drozd

Ce couple excentrique de peintres habite une roulotte de gitan et une «cabane» aux couleurs vives. De leur lopin de terre balayé par les vagues, on aperçoit le clocher des Saintes-Maries-de-la-Mer. Barrera est d'origine russe. Après de nombreuses fuites, plusieurs changements d'identité, un bref passage dans les services secrets pendant la guerre, et un séjour dans une prison marseillaise, il a ressenti le besoin d'une existence plus tranquille dans ce petit coin de Camargue, loin de l'agitation des villes. Inken Drozd est arrivée un beau jour devant la porte de sa cabane, à l'occasion de l'une des fameuses fêtes gitanes de Barrera. Elle n'en est jamais repartie. Tous deux partagent une conception philosophique et généreuse de la vie, accueillant les amis dans leur roulotte pour le thé ou l'apéritif, contemplant les flamants roses qui peuplent la lagune au coucher du soleil.

Dieses exzentrische Malerpaar lebt in einem bunt bemalten Zigeunerwagen und einer »cabane camarguaise« auf einem direkt am Meer gelegenen Grundstück, nur einen Steinwurf von der Kirche von Les Saintes-Maries-de-la-Mer entfernt. In die Provence verschlug es den gebürtigen Russen Barrera erst nach einem abenteuerlichen Leben: Er mußte mehrfach seinen Namen ändern, arbeitete während des Krieges für den britischen Geheimdienst, saß eine Zeitlang in Marseille im Gefängnis, um schließlich, getragen von dem Wunsch nach einem ruhigeren Leben, dem hektischen städtischen Treiben den Rücken zu kehren. Inken Drozd stand eines Tages, als gerade eines von Barreras spektakulären Zigeunerfesten im Gange war, vor der Tür seiner »cabane« – und blieb einfach dort. Beide sehen das Leben von der philosophischen Seite. Gäste sind stets willkommen und werden im Wohnwagen großzügig mit Tee bewirtet oder genießen bei einem verfrühten Aperitif den Blick auf die rosa Flamingos, die in der Abenddämmerung das Rhônedelta bevölkern.

Views of the caravan deliberately decorated in a pastiche of rococo
"gypsy" style. It is used as an occasional bedroom for the painters'
models who come to stay. Otherwise Inken considers it her "den",
where she can retire to read or write and not be disturbed.

La roulotte avec son décor pastiche du style «rococo gitan». Elle fait
occasionnellement office de chambre à coucher pour les modèles des
peintres. Le reste du temps, Inken la considère comme sa «tanière»,
où elle peut se retirer pour lire ou écrire sans être dérangée.

Der Wohnwagen ist mit einem eigenwilligen Sammelsurium von
»zigeunerhaften« Rokoko-Elementen eingerichtet. Er dient den
Modellen der beiden Maler bei gelegentlichen Aufenthalten als
Schlafzimmer. Ist der Wohnwagen frei, betrachtet Inken ihn als ihre
»Höhle«, in die sie sich zum ungestörten Lesen und Schreiben
zurückziehen kann.

Henri Aubanel still owns an imposing herd of semi-wild bulls that roam the marshlands of the Camargue, and the wardens who tend to them still ride the stocky little white horses known as the "camarguais". He lives, however, very simply in a traditional "cabane", the low, almost oval huts with high, thatched roofs, that are dotted about here and there in the Camargue. The "cabanes", such as this one, have their origins in the 19th century. Their structure is adapted to life on the marshy, mosquito-infested plain. In the thirties Henri Aubanel's marriage to Frédérique, the poet Mistral's god-daughter and daughter of the legendary gentleman bull breeder, Fulco Marquis de Baroncelli, brought together two of the most celebrated families in Provence. The famous herd became the "manade" Baroncelli-Aubanel, symbolic of both men's denial of their aristocratic birthright. Aubanel was greatly influenced by Baroncelli, who had adhered to the Romantic movement, and together they embraced the ideal of the simple outdoor life as breeders of fine bulls.

La cabane camarguaise d'Henri Aubanel

Henri Aubanel possède un imposant troupeau de taureaux en semi-liberté qui arpentent les marais sous la surveillance de gardians montant ces petits chevaux blancs et trapus qu'on appelle «camarguais». Il n'en vit pas moins très simplement dans sa «cabane»: ces petites chaumières basses traditionnelles, presque ovales, qui parsèment la Camargue. L'origine de la cabane telle qu'on la voit ici remonte au XIXe siècle. Sa structure est adaptée à la vie dans la plaine marécageuse infestée de moustiques. Dans les années trente, le mariage d'Henri et de Frédérique, filleule du poète Frédéric Mistral et fille du légendaire éleveur de taureaux le marquis Fulco de Baroncelli, a réuni les deux familles les plus célèbres de Camargue. Le fameux troupeau est devenu «la manade Baroncelli-Aubanel», symbole du peu de cas que faisaient les deux hommes de leur naissance aristocratique. Aubanel a été fortement influencé par Baroncelli, adepte du mouvement romantique. Tous deux ont adopté l'idéal d'une vie simple au grand air en se consacrant à l'élevage de taureaux de qualité.

Henri Aubanel besitzt noch immer eine eindrucksvolle Herde halbwilder Stiere, die sich in den Sumpfgebieten der Camargue frei bewegen. Ihre Hirten, die »gardians«, reiten noch heute die kleinen, aber stämmigen weißen Camargue-Pferde. Er selbst lebt allerdings sehr bescheiden in einer traditionellen »cabane«, einem der niedrigen, fast ovalen Häuschen mit hohem Schilfrohrdach, die man hier und dort in der Camargue noch findet. »Cabanes« wie die hier abgebildete entstanden im 19. Jahrhundert und sind ganz und gar auf das Leben in der sumpfigen, von Mückenschwärmen heimgesuchten Ebene ausgerichtet. In den dreißiger Jahren heiratete Henri Aubanel Frédérique, eine Patentochter des Dichters Mistral und Tochter des legendären hochherrschaftlichen Stierzüchters Fulco Marquis de Baroncelli, und vereinte damit zwei der bedeutendsten provenzalischen Familien. Die berühmte Stierherde wurde zur »manade Baroncelli-Aubanel«, zum Symbol für den Verzicht beider Männer auf ihre angestammten aristokratischen Vorrechte. Aubanel stand stark unter dem Einfluß des Romantikers Baroncelli, und gemeinsam verwirklichten sie das Ideal des einfachen Landlebens.

This low-lying ranch, painted a blinding white with Mediterranean chalk-wash, is home to the Colomb de Daunant. An ancient Provençal family, they continue to breed horses and the indigenous bulls which are reputed to be direct descendants of the bulls of Mycenae and Crete. Denys Colomb de Daunant is a respected personality who has written screenplays and books based on the art of "tauromachie", the bullfighting, in Camargue. His wife is a grand-daughter of Baroncelli. They live close to the land and their livestock, dependent upon the weather and unpredictable nature. Life at the "mas" can be tough: the climate is extreme, the humidity all-pervasive, and the mosquitoes a scourge. For 30 years the house had no electricity and very few modern conveniences. Its charm comes from its structure: the low, large rooms; the small windows under the eaves; the earthenware tiles on the roofs and the floor; all contribute to keeping the house cool during the torrid summers. The interiors are remarkable for their uncluttered purity and are reminiscent of Spain or Mexico rather than Provence.

Le Mas de Cacharel

Ce ranch bas, auquel les façades étincelantes blanchies à la chaux donnent une allure méditerranéenne, est la maison des Colomb de Daunant. Cette vieille famille provençale possède un élevage de chevaux et de taureaux camarguais qui seraient les descendants directs des taureaux de Mycène et de Crète. Denys Colomb de Daunant est une personnalité respectée de la région. Il est l'auteur de scénarios et de livres basés sur la tauromachie camarguaise. Avec sa femme, une petite fille du marquis de Baroncelli, ils vivent près de la terre et de leur bétail, dépendent du temps et de la nature imprévisibles. La vie au mas n'est pas toujours facile: le climat est rude, l'humidité et les moustiques sont omniprésents. Pendant trente ans, la maison n'avait même pas l'électricité et très peu de confort moderne. Tout son charme est dans son agencement: les grandes pièces basses de plafond, les petites fenêtres sous les auvents et les tomettes en terre cuite contribuent à conserver la fraîcheur de la maison pendant les mois d'été torrides. Les intérieurs, remarquables par leur pureté dépouillée, rappellent davantage l'Espagne ou le Mexique que la Provence.

Dieser tiefgelegene und mit blendend weißer Kalkfarbe gestrichene Hof wird von den Colomb de Daunant bewohnt. Die uralte provenzalische Familie züchtet noch heute Pferde und die heimischen Stiere, die angeblich direkte Nachfahren der Rinder von Mykene und Kreta sind. Denys Colomb de Daunant ist eine anerkannte Persönlichkeit der Region und hat mehrere Drehbücher und Bücher über die Tauromachien, die Stierspiele der Camargue, geschrieben. Gemeinsam mit seiner Frau, einer Enkelin Baroncellis, lebt er in enger Verbundenheit mit dem Land und seinen Tieren, in Abhängigkeit vom Wetter und den Launen der Natur. Das Leben auf dem Hof ist zuweilen hart: das Klima ist extrem, überall dringt Feuchtigkeit ein, und die Mücken sind eine Plage. Dreißig Jahre lang hatte das Haus weder Strom noch viel modernen Komfort. Sein Charme liegt in seiner Struktur, den niedrigen, weitläufigen Räumen, den kleinen Fenstern unter dem Dachvorsprung, den Dachpfannen und Bodenfliesen aus Keramik – alles trägt dazu bei, das Haus im glühend heißen Sommer kühl zu halten. Bei der Innenausstattung fällt die schnörkellose Schlichtheit auf, die eher an Spanien oder Mexiko als an die Provence erinnert.

Above and facing page: two views of Florian Colomb de Daunant's, Denys' son's, large main room. The bridles, stirrups and farm implements hanging from the whitewashed beams are a reminder to the billiard players that the Mas de Cacharel is very much a working ranch. The fabric for upholstery and curtains is a simple red cotton, or a bold gingham, perfectly suited to the masculine atmosphere.

Ci-dessus et page de droite: la grande pièce principale de la maison de Florian Colomb de Daunant, le fils de Denys. Les brides, les étriers et les outils de ferme suspendus aux poutres blanchies à la chaux rappellent aux joueurs de billard que le Mas de Cacharel est avant tout un lieu de travail. Les rideaux rouges et le vichy vif qui tapisse les meubles conviennent parfaitement à cette atmosphère masculine.

Oben und rechte Seite: zwei Ansichten des großen Hauptraumes der Wohnung von Denys Colomb de Daunants Sohn Florian. Die von den gekälkten Balken herabhängenden Trensen, Steigbügel und Gerätschaften erinnern die Billardspieler daran, daß der Mas de Cacharel in erster Linie ein bewirtschafteter Hof ist. Für Polster und Vorhänge verwendete man schlichten roten Baumwollstoff oder kühn gemustertes Leinengewebe, das zur maskulinen Atmosphäre sehr gut paßt.

Above: Denys' bedroom and study where he writes his books and screenplays. It is also home to what he refers to as "the world's most beautiful collection of objects of no value".
Facing page: a view of Florian's kitchen. Florian is dedicated to the protection of the ranch's traditional way of life and has chosen to preserve it by opening a charming, if simple, hotel on the property.

Ci-dessus: la chambre et le bureau de Denys, où il écrit ses livres et ses scénarios. Elle accueille également ce qu'il appelle «la plus belle collection du monde d'objets sans valeur».
Page de droite: la cuisine de Florian. Très attaché à la protection du mode de vie traditionnel du mas, Florian a choisi de le préserver en ouvrant un hôtel simple et charmant sur la propriété.

Oben: Denys' Schlaf- und Arbeitszimmer, in dem er seine Bücher und Drehbücher schreibt. Es beherbergt darüber hinaus das, was er selbst »der Welt schönste Sammlung völlig wertloser Gegenstände« nennt.
Rechte Seite: ein Blick in Florians Küche. Florian widmet sich mit großem Eifer dem Erhalt der traditionellen Lebensweise auf dem Hof und führt zu diesem Zweck ein zwar einfaches, jedoch sehr gemütliches Hotel auf dem Anwesen.

Jean Lafont breeds black bulls, hundreds of them; his herd, called "manade" in Provençal, is the oldest in Camargue and has been supplying Provençal bullfights since 1851 when it was founded by the Combet family. However, he is not just a bullfighting man. He is also the Director of the Nîmes opera house, a discerning collector and a celebrated horticulturalist. His home, where he has been living since 1963, is an extraordinary place, decorated and furnished with the help of Marie-Laure de Noailles. An aristocratic patron of the arts, she was both muse and financial backer to artists such as Man Ray, Le Corbusier and Balthus, thus playing a key role in the development of the avant-garde in France before and after the Second World War. Jean Lafont was a collector in his own right from the age of 20 and his house is a homage to his passion, being stuffed with incredibly varied pieces, so that every suite of rooms represents a particular style. The illustration below shows a detail of one of the century-old plane trees that surround the house.

Jean Lafont

Jean Lafont élève les taureaux noirs par centaines. Sa manade est la plus ancienne de Camargue et approvisionne les férias de Provence depuis 1851, date de sa création par la famille Combet. Toutefois, son activité ne s'arrête pas là: il est également directeur de l'opéra de Nîmes, collectionneur avisé et horticulteur renommé. La maison où il vit depuis 1963 est un lieu extraordinaire, décoré et meublé avec l'aide de Marie-Laure de Noailles. Cette mécène aristocratique, à la fois muse et soutien financier d'artistes tels que Man Ray, Le Corbusier et Balthus, a joué un rôle clef dans le développement de l'avant-garde en France avant et après la Seconde Guerre mondiale. Jean Lafont était collectionneur dès l'âge de 20 ans et sa maison est un hommage à sa passion: elle est pleine à craquer d'une incroyable variété d'objets, chaque enfilade de pièces représentant un style particulier. Le détail ci-dessous montre l'un des platanes centenaires qui entourent la maison.

Jean Lafont züchtet schwarze Stiere, und zwar zu Hunderten. Seine Herde, hier »manade« genannt, ist die älteste der Camargue und stellt seit ihrer Gründung 1851 durch die Familie Combet Tiere für provenzalische Stierkämpfe bereit. Lafont selbst ist jedoch nicht einfach nur ein stierkampfbegeisterter Züchter, sondern zudem Leiter des Opernhauses von Nîmes, ein anspruchsvoller Kunstsammler und renommierter Gartenexperte. Sein Haus, in dem er seit 1963 lebt, ist ein außergewöhnliches Gebäude, das er mit Hilfe von Marie-Laure de Noailles gestaltete und einrichtete. Als aristokratische Kunstmäzenin war sie Muse und zugleich finanzieller Rückhalt für Künstler wie Man Ray, Le Corbusier und Balthus und spielte damit eine zentrale Rolle in der Entwicklung der französischen Avantgarde vor und nach dem zweiten Weltkrieg. Jean Lafont ist seit seinem zwanzigsten Lebensjahr ein eigenwilliger Kunstsammler, und sein Haus belegt diese Leidenschaft mit einem Sammelsurium der verschiedensten Stücke. Jeder Raum des Hauses präsentiert sich in einem anderen Stil. Das Detail unten zeigt eine der jahrhundertealten Platanen, die das Haus umgeben.

Above and right: the art nouveau "Green Room", one of the three bedrooms on the first floor. The ceramic fireplace is by Muller and the "honeysuckle" wallpaper was designed by William Morris.

Ci-dessus et à droite: la chambre verte Art nouveau, l'une des trois chambres à coucher du premier étage. La cheminée en céramique est signée Muller et le papier peint «Chèvrefeuille» a été dessiné par William Morris.

Oben und rechts: das im Jugendstil eingerichtete »grüne Zimmer«, einer der drei Schlafräume im ersten Stock. Der aus Keramik gefertigte Kamin ist von Muller, die »Geißblatt«-Tapete ein Entwurf von William Morris.

On the previous pages: *a view of the spectacular glass conservatory, partly designed by the French sculptor César. The porcelain furniture is Sèvres, designed by a disciple of the painter Alfons Mucha. Beyond the conservatory lies the garden, internationally recognized as one of the finest examples of its kind.*
Above: *This room is entirely conceived in the "Gothic revival" style and pays homage to the "dilettante" 18th-century English collector Horace Walpole and his home Strawberry Hill.*
Detail right: *the Gothic bathroom.*

Double page précédente: *le somptueux jardin d'hiver, dessiné en partie par le sculpteur César. Le mobilier en porcelaine a été créé par un élève du peintre Alphonse Mucha pour la manufacture de Sèvres. Derrière, on aperçoit le jardin, un des plus beaux modèles du genre, qui s'étend jusqu'aux prés où paissent les taureaux.*
Ci-dessus: *Cette chambre est entièrement «Gothic revival», un hommage à Horace Walpole, collectionneur dilettante du XVIIIe siècle, et à sa maison Strawberry Hill.*
Détail à droite: *la salle de bains néo-gothique.*

Vorhergehende Doppelseite: *Blick in den prachtvollen, verglasten Wintergarten, der teilweise von dem französischen Bildhauer César entworfen wurde. Die Möbel aus Porzellan wurden in Sèvres nach Entwürfen eines Schülers des Malers Alfons Mucha gearbeitet. Hinter dem Wintergarten erstreckt sich der Garten – einer der schönsten seiner Art.*
Oben: *Dieser Raum ist vollständig im neugotischen Stil gehalten und ist eine Hommage an Horace Walpole, den englischen Kunstliebhaber und -sammler des 18. Jahrhunderts, und an sein Schloß Strawberry Hill.*
Detail rechts: *das neugotische Badezimmer.*

A view of the Héctor-Guimard-style salon, conceived to evoke the curvy aesthetics beloved of the man who designed the Paris metro entrances. It doubles as a library and office and includes Marie-Laure's mother's fine collection of rare books.
On the following pages: a view of the kitchen. Some of the furniture is by Jacques Majorelle, purchased from film director Louis Malle.

Le salon de style Héctor Guimard, qui évoque l'esthétique tout en courbes du créateur des entrées de métro parisien. Il sert également de bibliothèque et de bureau, et accueille la belle collection de livres rares de la mère de Marie-Laure.
Double page suivante: la cuisine. Certains des meubles sont signés Jacques Majorelle et ont été rachetés au cinéaste Louis Malle.

Blick in den Salon im Stil Héctor Guimards. Er greift die verschlungenen Linien auf, die Guimard bei der Gestaltung der Pariser Metroeingänge so gern verarbeitete. Der Raum dient als Bibliothek und zugleich als Büro und enthält wundervolle, seltene Bücher aus der Sammlung von Maire-Laures Mutter.
Folgende Doppelseite: Blick in die Küche. Einige der Möbel stammen von Jacques Majorelle; Lafont erwarb sie von dem französischen Filmregisseur Louis Malle.

Provence Interiors   Bruno Carles

The antiquarian Bruno Carles lives in the family home where he grew up and which he has since restored, infusing the house with a welcoming atmosphere, seeped in the charm of old Provence. The property, originally part of the Abbey of Psalmodie, is situated in the region known as "Petit Camargue". Life is lived largely out of doors: Bruno Carles has designed the garden on an intimate scale, to delight and surprise at every turn. The Anduze pottery he collects, wonderfully scented old roses and a small Louis XVI temple add interest to the Mediterranean flora that grows so freely here. Inside, the house has been painted in lively tones of ochre and yellow, spiked with shades of green. The floors are all in the traditional terracotta, and the panelling has been painted to bring a more modern feel to the graciously proportioned rooms. Bruno Carles edits a series based on 18th-century Provençal furniture. The detail below shows the stairway with its wrought iron balustrade.

Bruno Carles

L'antiquaire Bruno Carles vit dans la maison de famille où il a grandi et qu'il a depuis restaurée, y créant une atmosphère accueillante qui fleure bon la vieille Provence. La propriété, autrefois partie de l'abbaye de Psalmodie, est située dans «la petite Camargue». On y vit le plus souvent en plein air: Bruno Carles a dessiné un jardin aux dimensions intimes, où l'on sursaute avec ravissement à chaque tournant. La beauté de la végétation méditerranéenne qui y pousse librement est encore rehaussée par les poteries d'Anduze que Carles collectionne, un petit temple d'amour d'époque Louis XVI et des roses au parfum enivrant. L'intérieur de la maison est en tons vifs d'ocre et de jaune avec, ici et là, quelques touches de vert. Tous les sols sont en tomettes traditionnelles. Les boiseries ont été peintes pour donner une note plus moderne aux pièces aux proportions gracieuses. Bruno Carles crée lui-même de beaux meubles provençaux sur des modèles XVIIIème. Le détail ci-dessous montre l'escalier avec sa rampe en fer forgé.

Der Antiquitätenhändler Bruno Carles lebt im Haus seiner Familie, in dem er aufwuchs und das er mittlerweile renoviert hat. Dabei verlieh er dem Haus eine gastliche Atmosphäre, die noch den ganzen Charme der alten Provence in sich birgt. Das Anwesen, ursprünglich ein Teil der Abtei von Psalmody, liegt in der als »Petite Camargue« bezeichneten Gegend. Das Leben spielt sich im wesentlichen draußen ab: Den Garten hat Bruno Carles auf kleinem Raum angelegt; er bietet auf Schritt und Tritt hübsche, überraschende Ausblicke. Die Anduze-Keramik, die er sammelt, die herrlich duftenden alten Rosensorten und der kleine Tempel aus der Zeit Ludwigs XVI. lassen die ohnehin üppige mediterrane Flora noch schöner zur Geltung kommen. Im Innern ist das Haus in lebhaften Ocker- und Gelbtönen gestrichen und mit grünen Akzenten durchsetzt. Als Fußbodenbelag verwendete man traditionelle Terrakottafliesen, lediglich die Holzvertäfelungen wurden lackiert, um den großzügig geschnittenen Räumen ein modernes Flair zu geben. Unten ein Blick ins Treppenhaus mit seinem schmiedeeisernen Geländer.

Page 64: *in the background the oldest Anduze urn in Carles' collection, which dates from 1764.*
Above and right: *The vast birdcage in the garden shelters white doves. The wooden blinds and garden furniture have all been painted a Mediterranean blue.*

Page 64: *en arrière-plan, une poterie d'Anduze de 1764, la plus ancienne de la collection de Carles.*
Ci-dessus et à droite: *la volière du jardin qui abrite des colombes blanches. Tous les volets en bois et les meubles de jardin ont été peints en bleu méditerranéen.*

Seite 64: *links im Hintergrund eine Anduze-Amphore aus dem Jahr 1764, das älteste Stück in Carles' Sammlung.*
Oben und rechts: *Der riesige Vogelkäfig im Garten beherbergt weiße Tauben. Die hölzernen Fensterläden und Gartenmöbel sind in mediterranem Blau gestrichen.*

Provence Interiors   Bruno Carles

Below: the terrace with the table decked with autumnal offerings from the garden.
On the following pages: The highest room in the house has a ceiling painted in the spirit of the one in the nearby chapel of Saint-Michel de Frigolet. Bruno Carles collects "santibelli", typical Provençal religious figurines, which can be seen to the left of the picture and in the foreground.

Ci-dessous: la terrasse, avec sa table pleine de fruits d'automne cueillis dans le jardin.
Double page suivante: la pièce la plus haute de la maison avec un plafond peint inspiré de celui de la chapelle voisine de Saint-Michel de Frigolet. Sur la gauche et au premier plan, quelques pièces d'une collection de «santibelli», des statuettes religieuses typiquement provençales.

Unten: Die Terrasse mit einem herbstlichen Stilleben aus Gartenfrüchten.
Folgende Doppelseite: Die Decke des Raumes im obersten Stock ist mit Bildern im Stil der nahe gelegenen Kapelle Saint-Michel de Frigolet bemalt. Bruno Carles sammelt »santibelli«, typisch provenzalische Heiligenfiguren, die links im Bild und im Vordergrund zu sehen sind.

Nîmes, the sister-city of Arles, and yet on the wrong side of the Rhône to be officially included in Provence, was defined as very much a part of the region by the poet Frédéric Mistral. Hidden behind a 19th-century façade in the centre of the city lies the atypical loft-like apartment of Guillemette Goëlff. Designed by architect Jean-Michel Wilmotte, shown in the portrait, it is ultra-modern, an interesting experiment in proportion. The key concepts for the transformation of the building, situated only a stone's throw from the famous Roman arena, were light and transparency. The single unit, with its nine-metre high roof, is divided into more intimate spaces by frosted glass partitions or the play of the everpresent sunlight on columns and white walls. Here and there, a restored arch or a section of ancient stone bricks, highlighted by the white walls, recalls the original architecture of the building.

Guillemette Goëlff

Située sur la rive gauche du Rhône, Nîmes, ville sœur d'Arles, ne fait pas partie de la Provence officielle bien que le poète Frédéric Mistral l'inclue dans sa chère région. Au cœur de la ville, caché derrière une façade du XIXe siècle, se trouve le loft bien peu provençal de Guillemette Goëlff. Dessiné par l'architecte Jean-Michel Wilmotte, dont on peut voir le portrait ci-contre, l'espace ultramoderne constitue un intéressant jeu de proportions. Les concepts de base pour transformer l'édifice, situé à un jet de pierre des célèbres arènes romaines, étaient la lumière et la transparence. Le volume unique, avec son toit de neuf mètres de haut, est divisé en espaces plus intimes par des cloisons en verre dépoli ou par les rayons du soleil omniprésent qui dansent sur les colonnes et les murs blancs. Ici et là, une arche restaurée ou un fragment des anciens murs en briques mis en valeur par la blancheur des murs, rappellent la structure originale du bâtiment.

Nîmes, Schwesterstadt von Arles und doch jenseits der Rhône auf dem »falschen« Ufer, so daß es offiziell nicht zur Provence gerechnet wird, wurde von dem Dichter Frédéric Mistral dennoch sehr wohl als ein Teil von ihr aufgefaßt. Hinter einer Fassade aus dem 19. Jahrhundert liegt mitten in der Stadt die für die Provence völlig untypische Dachwohnung von Guillemette Goëlff. Das vom Architekten Jean-Michel Wilmotte, dessen Porträt auf dieser Seite zu sehen ist, entworfene Appartement ist hypermodern, ein interessantes Experiment mit Proportionen. Licht und Transparenz waren die Leitideen bei der Umgestaltung des Gebäudes, das nur einen Katzensprung vom berühmten römischen Amphitheater entfernt liegt. Der Hallenraum mit seinem neun Meter hohen Dachstuhl ist durch satinierte Glaswände und das Spiel des stets präsenten Sonnenlichts auf Säulen und weißen Wänden in kleinere Bereiche unterteilt. Hier und dort erinnert ein restaurierter Bogen oder ein Stück alten Mauerwerks, das vor der weißen Wand deutlich hervortritt, an die ursprüngliche Bauweise des Hauses.

Wilmotte built two blocks on the first floor that face each other across
the width of the apartment and provide the essential structure and
feeling of space. They house the bedrooms and are connected by a
walkway, shown in the detail right.

Au premier étage, Wilmotte a construit deux blocs qui se font face de
chaque côté de l'appartement et constituent la structure de base qui
définit l'espace. Ils abritent les chambres à coucher et sont reliés par
une passerelle montrée par le détail de droite.

Wilmotte errichtete zwei Blöcke im ersten Stock, die sich an den ent-
gegengesetzten Enden der Wohnung gegenüberliegen und den Raum
damit grundlegend gliedern. Sie enthalten die Schlafzimmer und sind
durch einen Gang verbunden, der auf dem Detail rechts zu sehen ist.

The minimal amount of furniture has been conceived either to blend
unobtrusively with the architectural project, as is the case with the
large, comfortable sofas swarthed in white linen, or to stand out
boldly, as this graphic Le Corbusier "chaise longue" does.

Le mobilier minimaliste a été choisi pour se fondre dans l'architecture
(grands sofas confortables drapés de lin blanc) ou pour s'en démar-
quer (chaise-longue aux lignes épurées, de Le Corbusier).

Die minimalistische Einrichtung wurde so angelegt, daß sie entweder
unaufdringlich mit den architektonischen Elementen verschmilzt, wie
die großen, bequemen Sofas mit dem weißen Leinenbezug, oder kühn
im Vordergrund steht, wie diese fast abstrakte Liege von Le Corbusier.

An American-Hungarian, born in Cuba and educated in France, Kathy Korvin feels most at home in this corner of the Alpilles where she has bought a tiny stone village house with a large garden. A talented jewellery designer, whose minimalist creations are in marked contrast to the prevalent Baroque aesthetic in jewellery design, she escapes to Provence as soon as her frantic Parisian life allows it. She loves the fact of her home being right in the middle of the village and part of the local life. Despite being situated very close to the writer Daudet's famous windmill, the setting for the Provençal classic "Letters from my Windmill", Kathy's world remains relatively untouched by tourism. The open market on the square and the little shops function just as they always have done; everybody knows everybody else and summer days are spent tending to the garden which she created from an empty plot of land.

Kathy Korvin

C'est dans ce petit coin des Alpilles que Kathy Korvin, une Américano-Hongroise née à Cuba et élevée en France, se sent le plus chez elle. Elle y a acheté une minuscule maison de village avec un grand jardin. Talentueuse créatrice de bijoux dont les réalisations minimalistes contrastent avec l'esthétique baroque qui prévaut actuellement en matière de joaillerie, elle s'échappe en Provence dès que la frénésie de sa vie parisienne le lui permet. Elle est ravie que sa maison se trouve en plein village et participe ainsi à la vie locale. Bien que situé à deux pas du célèbre moulin d'Alphonse Daudet, le monde de Kathy est relativement peu affecté par le tourisme. Dans le village, tout le monde se connaît. Le marché sur la place et les petits commerces fonctionnent comme ils l'ont toujours fait et Kathy passe ses journées d'été à s'occuper du jardin qu'elle a créé de toutes pièces.

Kathy Korvin, eine auf Kuba geborene und in Frankreich erzogene Amerikanerin ungarischer Abstammung, fühlt sich in dieser Ecke der Alpilles, wo sie ein winziges steinernes Dorfhaus mit großem Garten erstanden hat, ausgesprochen wohl. Sie ist eine begabte Schmuckdesignerin, deren minimalistische Kreationen in deutlichem Gegensatz zum vorherrschenden barocken Geschmack der gängigen Schmuckproduktion stehen. Sooft es ihr hektisches Pariser Leben erlaubt, flieht sie in die Provence. Ihr gefällt es, daß ihr Haus mitten im Ort steht und Teil des dörflichen Lebens ist. Auch wenn sie sehr nahe bei Daudets berühmter Windmühle wohnt, dem Schauplatz des provenzalischen Klassikers »Briefe aus meiner Mühle«, bleibt Kathys Welt von Touristen weitgehend verschont. Der Wochenmarkt auf dem Platz und die kleinen Geschäfte laufen so ab, wie sie es seit jeher tun: jeder kennt jeden, und an Sommertagen pflegt Kathy ihren Garten, den sie quasi aus dem Nichts geschaffen hat.

Above: a view of the beamed downstairs living room, dominated by the gracious stone fireplace whose presence in this humble village cottage remains a mystery. The house is kept simply but gaily furnished. These sculptures and the heart painting are by Kathy's boyfriend, Australian artist Mark Stuart.
Facing page: another view of the main room with a twisted wire heart chandelier over the dining-table. The fabrics include a number of Provençal "boutis" as well as kilims and embroidered fabric brought back from their travels.

Ci-dessus: le salon du rez-de-chaussée avec ses poutres apparentes. Il est dominé par une élégante cheminée en pierre dont la présence dans cette humble maison de village reste un mystère. Le décor de la maison est simple et gai. Les sculptures et le tableau représentant un cœur sont l'œuvre du compagnon de Kathy, l'artiste australien Mark Stuart.
Page de droite: une autre vue de la pièce principale avec un lustre en métal noué en forme de cœur au-dessus de la table. Partout, des boutis provençaux, des kilims et des étoffes brodées rapportées de voyages.

Oben: Blick in das von einer Balkendecke überspannte Wohnzimmer im Erdgeschoß, das von einem schönen steinernen Kamin beherrscht wird, von dem niemand sagen kann, wie er in dieses bescheidene Dorfhäuschen geraten sein mag. Das Haus ist einfach, aber freundlich eingerichtet. Die Skulpturen und das Herzbild stammen von Kathys Lebensgefährten, dem australischen Künstler Mark Stuart.
Rechte Seite: Ein weiterer Blick in den Hauptraum mit einem Herzen aus verzwirntem Draht, das über dem Eßtisch als Kerzenhalter dient. Die Stoffe sind zum Teil provenzalische »boutis«, neben Kelims und bestickten Stoffen, die Kathy von ihren Reisen mitgebracht hat.

On the slopes of those craggy little mountains know as the Alpilles, the Pellens raise fine horses, which are then bought and exported as far afield as Britain and Germany. Gerald Pellen has horses in his blood and is known not only as an excellent breeder but also as one of the best "rejoneadores" in Provence. He has recently initiated his daughter Patricia into the art of mounted bullfighting and she is one of the very few women to be recognized as a "rejoneadora". On a "corrida" day, a day when bullfights are held, father and daughter dress up in the traditional costume, and travel with their horses to whichever local town is staging the "feria". Pellen has even been accorded the rare honour, as a Provençal, of being invited to display his talents in Spain, home of all bullfighting. At Pellen's family-run stables life is lived according to the needs of the horses: caring for them, breaking them in, training them or practising in the small bullring on the farm, pitting highly strung throughbreds against young bulls.

Gerald Pellen

On vient d'Angleterre et d'Allemagne pour acheter les beaux chevaux des Pellen élevés sur les versants escarpés des Alpilles. Gerald Pellen a les chevaux dans le sang. Ce n'est pas seulement un excellent éleveur mais également le meilleur «rejoneador» de Provence. Il a initié sa fille Patricia à l'art de toréer à cheval et c'est l'une des rares femmes à s'être imposée dans cette profession. Les jours de corrida, on peut voir père et fille faire leur entrée en tenue traditionnelle et accompagnés de leurs montures dans la ville qui accueille la féria. Pellen a même eu le grand honneur, rare pour un Provençal, d'être invité à montrer ses talents en Espagne, patrie de la tauromachie. Dans les écuries des Pellen, la vie est réglée en fonction des besoins des chevaux: il faut les bouchonner, les dresser et les entraîner sur la petite arène du haras, où des pur-sang très nerveux rencontrent de jeunes taureaux.

An den Hängen des zerklüfteten kleinen Alpilles-Gebirges züchtet die Familie Pellen Rassepferde, die bis nach Großbritannien und Deutschland verkauft werden. Gerald Pellen liegen Pferde sozusagen im Blut. Er ist nicht nur ein erfolgreicher Züchter, sondern außerdem auch einer der besten »rejoneadores« der Provence. Auch seine Tochter Patricia hat er in die Kunst des berittenen Stierkampfes eingeführt. Sie wurde als eine von sehr wenigen Frauen mittlerweile selbst als »rejoneadora« zugelassen. Wenn eine Corrida ansteht, ziehen Vater und Tochter die traditionellen Trachten an und fahren mit ihren Pferden zu dem jeweiligen Ort, wo die »feria« stattfindet. Pellen wurde sogar eingeladen, in Spanien, dem Mutterland des Stierkampfes, seine Künste vorzuführen – eine für einen Provenzalen erstaunliche Ehre. In den von der Familie Pellen geführten Ställen orientiert sich das Leben ganz an den Bedürfnissen der Pferde. Man füttert und pflegt sie, reitet sie zu, trainiert sie oder übt in der kleinen Arena auf dem Hof, wo man nervöse Vollblüter gegen junge Stiere antreten läßt.

Above: the entrance hall, where boots and hunting guns stand next to the door, and where trophies and the elaborately decorated "banderillas" are displayed.
Detail right: Patricia's bullfighting costume, a traditional tight-fitting jacket and tie.

Ci-dessus: on dépose ses bottes et ses fusils de chasse près de la porte de l'entrée, où sont exposés trophées et banderilles ouvragées.
Détail de droite: la tenue de «rejoneadora de Patricia», une veste cintrée et une cravate.

Oben: die Eingangshalle, wo Stiefel und Jagdgewehre direkt neben der Tür stehen und wo Trophäen sowie die prächtig dekorierten Banderillas zur Schau gestellt werden.
Detail rechts: Patricias Stierkampfkostüm. Es besteht aus einer eng anliegenden Jacke und einer Krawatte.

The bedroom on the first floor, decorated with florid posters advertising different "corridas". Gerald's bullfighter's cape in the traditional bright pink and deep yellow echoes the ancient "souleiado" bedspread.

La chambre du premier étage, décorée d'affiches de corridas. La cape traditionnelle rose vif et jaune sombre de Gerald est en harmonie avec le «souleiado» ancien du dessus-de-lit.

Im Schlafzimmer im ersten Stock hängen grellbunte Plakate mit Ankündigungen diverser Corridas. Geralds Stierkampfcape, traditionell in leuchtendem Pink und Gelb, paßt zum alten »Souleiado«-Bettüberwurf.

Conran is undoubtedly one of the most important influences on the aesthetics of contemporary interiors. Since he opened the first Habitat in London in 1964, and with his instinctive taste for good, strong design in the home, he has changed the way people perceive decoration. Conran managed to impose a "continental" aesthetic on the insular English in the sixties. France, and the South in particular, has long been an inspiration. The beautifully restored "Mas de Brunélys" near Tarascon is an excercise in "savoire-vivre": very French but very Conran. The house was built in the early 19th century to the design of an Italian count, who endowed the construction with a particular graciousness. The Conrans bought it with 200 acres of olive groves and arable land, which they still allow to be cultivated by the local farmer.

Sir Terence Conran

L'Anglais Sir Terence Conran est sans doute l'un de ceux qui ont le plus influencé la décoration contemporaine. Depuis l'ouverture du premier Habitat en 1964 à Londres, son sens inné d'un design aux lignes fortes a transformé la manière dont les gens conçoivent leurs intérieurs. Dans les années soixante, il est parvenu à imposer une esthétique «continentale» aux Anglais pourtant insulaires. La France et le Sud en particulier, l'inspirent depuis longtemps. Le superbe Mas de Brunélys qu'il a restauré près de Tarascon est une leçon de savoir-vivre, à la fois très français et très «Conran». La maison a été construite au début du XIXe siècle selon les plans d'un comte italien qui a su lui insuffler une certaine grâce. Les Conran l'ont achetée avec 80 hectares d'oliveraies et de terre arable, qui sont encore cultivées par un fermier de la région.

Conran gehört zweifellos zu den Designern, die großen Einfluß auf die zeitgenössische Innenarchitektur ausüben. Seit er 1964 das erste Habitat-Geschäft in London eröffnete, hat er mit seinem Instinkt für gutes, kraftvolles Wohndesign die Rolle der Innenarchitektur nachhaltig verändert. In den sechziger Jahren gelang es Conran, den Briten die »kontinentale« Ästhetik nahezubringen. Frankreich, vor allem der Süden, ist für ihn seit langem eine Quelle der Inspiration. Der wunderschön restaurierte Mas de Brunélys in der Nähe von Tarascon ist ein Modell des »Savoir-vivre«, sehr französisch und zugleich eindeutig ein Conran. Das Haus wurde im frühen 19. Jahrhundert nach Entwürfen eines italienischen Grafen erbaut, der ihm eine ausgesprochen anmutige Note verlieh. Die Conrans kauften das Anwesen zusammen mit 80 Hektar Olivenhainen und Ackerland, die nach wie vor von einem Bauern des Dorfes bewirtschaftet werden.

Facing page: The garden was conceived by Sir Terence. Its strong simple lines are characteristic of his work. The garden is planted with a wide variety of Mediterranean plants that can survive the hot summers and stony terrain. The pond is one of the main features, and water cascades down to either side of the stone steps.
Above: the simple façade of one of the wings, previously a farm building. The luxuriant vine-covered trellis shades the doorway.

Page de gauche: le jardin dessiné par Sir Terence. Ses lignes simples et nettes sont typiques du style Conran. Il est planté d'une grande variété de plantes méditerranéennes adaptées au terrain rocailleux et aux étés torrides. Le bassin est l'un des principaux attraits du jardin, l'eau y tombant en cascade de chaque côté des marches en pierre.
Ci-dessus: la façade sobre de l'ancien bâtiment de ferme devenu une des ailes de la maison. Une tonnelle luxuriante plonge le pas de la porte dans une ombre fraîche.

Linke Seite: Der Garten wurde von Sir Terence selbst entworfen. Die starken, einfachen Linien sind typisch für seine Arbeiten. Die Bepflanzung umfaßt eine reiche Mittelmeervegetation, die heiße Sommer ebenso verträgt wie den steinigen Boden. Ein wesentliches Element ist der Teich, dessen Wasser zu beiden Seiten neben der Steintreppe abfließt.
Oben: die schlichte Fassade eines ehemals bewirtschafteten Gebäudeflügels. Die prächtige Laube überschattet den Eingang.

The salon, built in one of the wings. This room, with its low, beamed ceiling and the big fireplace in local stone, is a favourite after-dinner spot. Even in summer, the log fire is often lit late in the evening. Two Provençal "boutis" have been thrown over the simple white sofas from The Conran Shop.

Le salon, aménagé dans l'une des ailes. C'est dans cette pièce au plafond bas, aux poutres apparentes et à la grande cheminée en pierre locale que l'on se retire après le dîner. Même l'été, un feu y brûle jusque tard dans la soirée. Deux boutis provençaux ont été jetés sur de simples sofas blancs provenant de la boutique Conran.

Der Salon in einem der Seitenflügel. In diesem Raum mit seiner niedrigen Balkendecke und dem großen Kamin aus hiesigem Stein sitzt man nach dem Abendessen gemütlich beisammen. Selbst im Sommer brennt im Kamin oft bis spät in die Nacht ein Feuer. Zwei provenzalische »Boutis«-Decken wurden über zwei schlichte weiße Sofas aus »The Conran Shop« geworfen.

Provence Interiors   Sir Terence Conran

Detail right: one of the traditional French wicker baskets that Conran has always admired.
Below: the perspective from the pale yellow dining-room. A few well chosen antiques, such as the carved butcher's table shown, co-habit happily with pieces Conran has designed himself. His philosophy has always been that furniture must be both practical and attractive to be considered good design; and this premise is of course applicable to furniture and utensils of any epoch.

Détail de droite: un de ces paniers en osier traditionnels que Conran a toujours admirés.
Ci-dessous: la perspective depuis la salle à manger jaune pâle. Quelques antiquités bien choisies, comme la table de boucher en bois sculpté, cohabitent avec des meubles dessinés par Conran lui-même. Pour lui, un objet réussi, quelle qu'en soit l'époque, doit être à la fois beau et fonctionnel.

Detail rechts: einer der traditionsreichen französischen Weidenkörbe, die Conran seit langem liebt.
Unten: Blick aus dem hellgelben Eßzimmer. Wenige ausgewählte Antiquitäten wie der abgebildete geschnitzte Metzgertisch fügen sich nahtlos zwischen Möbel ein, die nach Conrans eigenen Entwürfen gefertigt wurden. Seine Philosophie ist seit jeher, daß Möbel sowohl praktisch als auch schön sein müssen, um als gutes Design zu gelten. Dies gilt natürlich für Möbel und Gebrauchsgegenstände aus jeder Epoche.

Above and detail right: the kitchen, the heart of the house, perfectly equipped for Conran's culinary sessions. Guests are often invited to join in the preparations as cooking is one of the Conran's great passions. The mirrors above the counter are placed to reflect all the bounty of the Alpilles, which is a particularily fertile corner of Provence.
Facing page: the bedroom which has something of an exotic air with its blue Indian "dhurri" and tiger painting, but which otherwise is as simply furnished as the rest of the house.

Ci-dessus et détail de droite: la cuisine, cœur de la maison, parfaitement équipée pour les séances culinaires de Conran. Les invités participent souvent aux préparatifs des repas, la cuisine étant l'une des grandes passions de Sir Terence. Les miroirs au-dessus du comptoir reflètent le paysage généreux des Alpilles, ce petit coin de Provence particulièrement fertile.
Page de droite: La chambre est meublée aussi sobrement que le reste de la maison, mais dégage un petit parfum d'exotisme avec des «dhurris» indiens et un tableau représentant un tigre.

Oben und Detail rechts: Die Küche, das Herzstück des Hauses, ist bestens ausgerüstet für Conrans kulinarische Ambitionen. Gäste werden häufig eingeladen, den Vorbereitungen beizuwohnen, denn Kochen ist eine von Conrans großen Leidenschaften. Der Spiegel über dem Tresen verdoppelt die Schönheit der Alpilles, einer der fruchtbarsten Gegenden der Provence.
Rechte Seite: Das Schlafzimmer gewinnt seine leicht exotische Note durch den blauen indischen Dhurri-Teppich und das Tigerbild. Es ist ansonsten jedoch genauso schlicht eingerichtet wie der Rest des Hauses.

This Renaissance construction, added to and beautified in the 17th and 18th centuries, is a poetic expression of Irène and Giorgio's extraordinary taste. Walls awash with colour, uneven floors, unexpected objects adapted to all sorts of domestic uses for which they were not intended, antique fabrics, fascinating plays on light... Their home is the reflection of their innate talent for the creation of an atmosphere. He is a film producer and script-writer, who mockingly refers to himself as "a frustrated decorator" and who took great pleasure in producing the subtle pigment effects on the walls. She was a brilliant fashion director at French "Vogue" and now advises Japanese designer, Yohji Yamamoto. Together they have lovingly restored the "bastide", discovered one day when the mistral was particularly wicked, allowing the gracious proportions, the weathered building materials, the eccentric distribution to speak for themselves.

Irène et Giorgio Silvagni

Cette demeure de la Renaissance, agrandie et embellie au XVIIe et XVIIIe siècles, est l'expression poétique du goût extraordinaire d'Irène et de Giorgio Silvagni. Les murs inondés de couleur, les sols inégaux, les objets insolites, les étoffes anciennes, les fantastiques jeux de lumière... tout dans leur intérieur reflète leur talent inné pour créer une atmosphère. Giorgio est un producteur de cinéma et un scénariste qui se qualifie lui-même par dérision de «décorateur frustré». Il a pris un grand plaisir à produire les effets subtils de pigments sur les murs. Après une brillante carrière de rédactrice de mode pour le «Vogue» français, Irène conseille désormais le styliste japonais Yohji Yamamoto. Ensemble, ils ont restauré avec amour cette bastide découverte un jour où le mistral était particulièrement mauvais et laissé les belles proportions, les matières patinées par le temps et la distribution excentrique des pièces parler d'elles-mêmes.

Dieses im 17. und 18. Jahrhundert erweiterte und verschönerte Renaissancegebäude ist poetischer Ausdruck von Irènes und Giorgios exzellentem Geschmack: farbüberflutete Wände, unebene Fußböden, mannigfache Gegenstände, die unerwartet häuslichen Zwecken dienen, für die sie gar nicht gedacht waren, schöne alte Stoffe, faszinierende Lichtspiele – alles in ihrem Heim bezeugt ihr angeborenes Talent, Atmosphäre zu schaffen. Giorgio ist Filmproduzent und Drehbuchautor und bezeichnet sich selbst augenzwinkernd als einen »verhinderten Maler«. Mit großem Vergnügen schuf er die Pigmenteffekte auf den Wänden. Irène leitete früher das Moderessort der französischen Zeitschrift «Vogue» und ist inzwischen Beraterin des japanischen Modeschöpfers Yohji Yamamoto. Gemeinsam mit ihrem Mann restaurierte sie mit viel Liebe die »bastide«. Dabei ließen sie die anmutigen Proportionen, wettergegerbten Baustoffe und die ausgefallene Raumaufteilung für sich selbst sprechen.

Page 91: *a view of the ochre dining-room with its chandelier improvised out of tri-coloured lanterns.*
On the previous pages: *a view of the pink salon, in the last of the evening sunlight. The large comfortable sofas are covered in striped mattress ticking. The floor is in the rounded pebbles typical of the region. The two stone fountains on either side of the fireplace are Renaissance.*
Above and facing page: *two views of the master bedroom, with its periwinkle blue walls and the ancient red tiled floor. The alcove, which was also an original feature of the house, contains a large table with a quilted Provençal "boutis" thrown over it.*

Page 91: *la salle à manger ocre avec son lustre improvisé avec des lanternes tricolores.*
Double page précédente: *le salon rose sous les derniers feux du coucher de soleil. Les grands sofas profonds sont recouverts de toile à matelas rayée. Le sol est incrusté de galets de la région. Les deux fontaines en pierre de chaque côté de la cheminée datent de la Renaissance.*
Ci-dessus et page de droite: *la chambre de maître, avec ses murs bleu pervenche et son sol en tomettes anciennes. L'alcôve, également d'origine, accueille une grande table sur laquelle est jeté un boutis provençal matelassé.*

Seite 91: *Blick in das ockerfarbene Eßzimmer. Der Kerzenleuchter ist aus dreifarbigen Laternen zusammengesetzt.*
Vorhergehende Doppelseite: *Blick in den rötlichen Salon im letzten Sonnenlicht. Die ausladenden, gemütlichen Sofas sind mit gestreiftem Matratzendrillich bezogen. Der Fußboden besteht aus den für diese Gegend typischen runden Kieseln. Die beiden Steinbecken rechts und links des Kamins sind echte Renaissancestücke.*
Oben und rechte Seite: *Zwei Ansichten des Elternschlafzimmers mit den blauvioletten Wänden und dem alten roten Fliesenboden. Der Alkoven gehörte zur Originaleinrichtung des Hauses und enthält einen großen Tisch, über den ein provenzalischer »Boutis«-Quilt gebreitet ist.*

Facing page: a view of the blue and white "chess-board" bathroom, situated in an alcove off the master bedroom. The free-standing bath has improvised curtains made of antique embroidered linen sheets.
Above: the guest bedroom, housed in what used to be the stable.

Page de gauche: la salle de bains en damier bleu et blanc, nichée dans une alcôve de la chambre de maître. Les rideaux improvisés de la baignoire sur pieds sont d'anciens draps de lin brodés.
Ci-dessus: la chambre d'amis dans l'ancienne écurie.

Linke Seite: Blick in das blauweiß gewürfelte Badezimmer, das in einer Nische hinter dem Schlafzimmer liegt. Die freistehende Wanne hat improvisierte Vorhänge aus alten bestickten Leinenbahnen.
Oben: das Gästezimmer im früheren Stall.

This rural "mas" lies not far from Tarascon, the celebrated birthplace of the imaginary Tartarin de Tarascon (the writer Alphone Daudet's comic pastiche of the Provençal rustic). Here, a well-known Parisian restaurateur has created a romantic bolt-hole, buried among the orchards of this particularly pretty corner of the lowlands. The inherent simplicity of the house has intentionally been left to shine through. The walls are limewashed with veils of intense colour, but the uneven floors, rough plaster, stairs worn down by many years of footsteps, and the irregular stone work have been allowed to remain, infusing the house with a charm all of its own. The restoration was essentially a case of peeling away layers of previous attempts at decoration in order to reveal the bones of the 18th-century structure.

Un mas en Provence

Ce mas de campagne se trouve près de Tarascon, lieu de naissance du fameux Tartarin, ce rustre provençal imaginé par Alphonse Daudet. Sa propriétaire, une célèbre restauratrice parisienne, en a fait un refuge romantique, enfoui entre les vergers de ce petit coin particulièrement charmant des basses terres. Elle a choisi de préserver la simplicité inhérente à la bâtisse: si les murs ont été passés à la chaux avec un voile de couleurs intenses, les parquets inégaux, le plâtre brut, les escaliers usés par le temps et la maçonnerie grossière sont restés tels quels, conférant à la maison un charme bien particulier. La restauration a simplement consisté à ôter les unes après les autres les tentatives de décoration précédentes afin de mettre à nu les murs du XVIIIe siècle.

Der bäuerliche »mas« liegt ganz in der Nähe von Tarascon, dem berühmten Geburtsort der Romanfigur Tartarin, Alphonse Daudets komischer Parodie auf die provenzalischen Bauern. Hier, in diesem besonders schönen Teil der Ebene, hat eine bekannte Pariser Gastronomin sich zwischen Obstgärten einen romantischen Schlupfwinkel geschaffen. Bewußt wurde bei der Restaurierung die ursprüngliche Schlichtheit des Hauses bewahrt. Die Wände sind mit Kalkfarben in satten Tönen gestrichen, doch die unebenen Fußböden, der Rauhputz, die in langen Jahren von vielen Füßen abgetretene Treppe und das unregelmäßige Mauerwerk wurden belassen und geben dem Haus einen ganz eigenen Charme. Die Restaurierungsarbeiten bestanden im wesentlichen darin, diverse Schichten früherer Dekorationen abzukratzen, um darunter das »Gerippe« des aus dem 18. Jahrhundert stammenden Gebäudes freizulegen.

On the previous pages: the canary-yellow kitchen showing the fireplace that is dated 1760.
Above: the master bedroom, built in what was the hayloft. It occupies the same volume of space as the living room, which is directly underneath it and was in turn converted from the stables. The cupboard doors and the partition separating the bathroom from the rest of the room are made from the recycled wooden blinds of a local chateau.

Double page précédente: la cuisine jaune canari et la cheminée qui date de 1760.
Ci-dessus: la chambre de maître installée dans l'ancien grenier à foin. Elle occupe le même volume que le salon, situé juste en dessous dans ce qui étaient autrefois les écuries. Les portes des placards et la cloison qui séparent la salle de bains de la chambre sont d'anciens volets en bois provenant d'un château des environs.

Vorhergehende Doppelseite: Die kanariengelbe Küche besitzt noch einen Originalkamin aus dem Jahr 1760.
Oben: Das Schlafzimmer wurde im ehemaligen Heuboden eingerichtet und ist genauso geräumig wie das unmittelbar darunter gelegene Wohnzimmer, das seinerseits den Platz eines früheren Stalls einnimmt. Für die Schranktüren und die Trennwände zwischen dem Bad und dem übrigen Raum wurden hölzerne Fensterläden eines nahe gelegenen Schlosses verwendet.

Below: The sink has been set in an antique draper's table, bought from the antique dealer Xavier Nicod at L'Isle-sur-la-Sorgue (see pp. 144–149). He was a keen accomplice in the furnishing of this "mas". The lady of the house adores flea markets, antique shops, and hunting for new bits and pieces for her home, and knows the local "brocantes", the secondhand markets and stores, by heart.

Ci-dessous: l'évier est encastré dans une table de drapier, achetée à l'Isle-sur-la-Sorgue chez l'antiquaire Xavier Nicod (voir pp. 144–149), un complice qui a fortement contribué à meubler le mas. La maîtresse de maison raffole des marchés aux puces et des boutiques d'antiquité. Chinant sans cesse de nouveaux objets pour son intérieur, elle connaît toutes les brocantes de la région sur le bout des doigts.

Unten: Das Waschbecken wurde in einen alten Stoffhändlertisch eingelassen, den die Hausbesitzerin bei dem Antiquitätenhändler Xavier Nicod in L'Isle-sur-la-Sorgue erstand (s. S. 144–149). Er war ihr bei der Einrichtung ihres »mas« sehr behilflich. Sie liebt Flohmärkte und Trödelläden und ist stets auf der Jagd nach neuen Stücken für ihr Haus. Die örtlichen «brocantes», die Trödelläden und -märkte, sind ihr alle bestens vertraut.

Emile Garcin is probably Provence's most well-loved estate agent, who has put a good many clients on the right road to buying a house in this region, thus indirectly making a fair amount of dreams come true. His own house, a repository for his beloved collections of objects, has enormous importance for him. Decorated in a warm and unaffected style, painted ochre, mustard and cream, the tones close to the heart of any Provençal, it serves as a backdrop to a great many accumulations. Among these are bears, an army of toy soldiers and a fleet of model cars. In the dining-room, a large wall is entirely covered with a valuable collection of earthenware plates, including the celebrated "terre mêlée" of Apt and "barbotines" in the spirit of 16th-century potter Bernard Palissy, famous for his gothic imagination.

Emile Garcin

Emile Garcin est probablement l'agent immobilier le plus populaire de Provence: il a aidé bon nombre de clients à trouver une maison dans cette région magique, contribuant ainsi à la concrétisation de nombreux rêves. Il attache une importance considérable à sa propre maison. Décorée dans un style chaleureux et sans prétention, peinte en ocre, moutarde et blanc cassé, les tons chers au cœur de tous les provençaux, elle sert de toile de fond à ses chères collections d'objets, qui incluent des ours, des modèles réduits de voitures et une armée de soldats de plomb. Un mur entier de la salle à manger est tapissé de sa précieuse collection d'assiettes en faïence, notamment les célèbres «terre mêlée» d'Apt et des «barbotines» dans l'esprit gothique du céramiste du XVIe siècle, Bernard Palissy.

Emile Garcin dürfte Frankreichs beliebtester Immobilienmakler sein. Er hat zahlreichen Kunden zu einem Grundbesitz in dieser magischen Region verholfen und damit indirekt zur Verwirklichung vieler Wunschträume beigetragen. Sein eigenes Haus ist für ihn, nicht zuletzt als Schatzkammer seiner geliebten Sammlungen, von immenser Bedeutung. In einem warmen, unprätentiösen Stil eingerichtet, die Wände in Ocker, Senf und Creme gestrichen – Farben, die das Herz jedes Provenzalen höher schlagen lassen – dient es als Rahmen für die vielen Sammlerstücke, darunter jede Menge Bären, eine ganze Armee von Zinnsoldaten und ein regelrechter Fuhrpark von Modellautos. Im Eßzimmer ist eine große Wand vollständig mit kostbaren Keramiktellern bedeckt, darunter die berühmte »terre mêlée« aus Apt und »barbotines« im Stil des Töpfers Bernard Palissy, der im 16. Jahrhundert für seine grotesken Figuren bekannt war.

Page 105: the façade of the manor, originally a 17th-century construction, and embellished in the 18th and 19th centuries.
Above: The billiard table dominates the beamed study, where various collections fight for space in a glorious example of fortuitous juxtaposition. Garcin collects as he goes about his work, which involves constant comings and goings across the region in order to restore and sell houses.

Page 105: la façade du manoir, une construction du XVIIe siècle, embellie au XVIIIe et XIXe siècles.
Ci-dessus: le bureau aux poutres apparentes où trône un billard dans un joyeux foisonnement de collections de toutes sortes. Garcin, qui sillonne la région pour restaurer ou vendre des maisons, les constitue au rythme de ses allées et venues professionnelles.

Seite 105: die Fassade des Landhauses, das im 17. Jahrhundert erbaut und im 18. und 19. Jahrhundert erneuert wurde.
Oben: Der Billardtisch dominiert das von einer Balkendecke überspannte Arbeitszimmer, in dem sich mehrere Sammlungen den Platz streitig machen und in einem fruchtbaren Nebeneinander gegenseitig ergänzen. Garcin sammelt sozusagen nebenbei, wenn ihn seine Arbeit kreuz und quer durch die Region führt, um Häuser zu restaurieren oder zu verkaufen.

Below: *the kitchen, with its bouquets of local aromatics hanging from the beams. The wicker baskets, fitted under the work surfaces are used as a rather more attractive interpretation of conventional kitchen drawers. Emile Garcin is something of a gourmet and even keeps the empty bottles of very good wine as souvenirs of particularly successful dinner parties.*
On the following pages: *Garcin designed the shelves himself, in order to display the pottery plate collection.*

Ci-dessous: *la cuisine, avec ses bouquets de plantes aromatiques locales suspendus aux poutres. Les paniers en osier sous le plan de travail offrent une alternative charmante aux tiroirs de cuisine. Fin gourmet, Emile Garcin conserve même les cadavres de grands crûs en souvenir de dîners particulièrement réussis.*
Double page suivante: *Garcin a lui-même dessiné les étagères pour présenter sa collection d'assiettes en faïence.*

Unten: *In der Küche hängen die Kräuter der Provence gebündelt von den Deckenbalken. Die unter der Arbeitsplatte angebrachten Weidenkörbe sind eine attraktive Variante der üblichen Küchenschubladen. Emile Garcin ißt gern gut und bewahrt die leeren Flaschen ausgezeichneter Weine auf als Erinnerung an besonders gelungene Festessen.*
Folgende Doppelseite: *Die Regalwand hat Garcin selbst entworfen, um seine Sammlung von Keramiktellern unterbringen zu können.*

One of the world's most sought after decorators, Jacques Grange does not spend as much time in his converted farmhouse near Saint-Rémy-de-Provence as he would like to. This is a great pity because the house is a real home: simple, comfortable and filled with truly inspiring pieces, which surprise or amuse but never overwhelm. It is a Provençal house that has been put together with a sense of humour and a sense of place. The garden is on a human scale, filled with fruit trees and flowers for picking. A strategically placed bench provides exactly the right spot to sit and admire the view. Inside, there are straw hats a-plenty, wicker baskets from the local shop and piles of books. In the well stocked larder, home made jam and "tapenade" are juxtaposed with piles of the local colourful ceramics. There is an open fire for grilling the dinner, to be then eaten at the kitchen table. In short, the house is a delight to live in and although it might well not be Grange's grandest project, it is certainly his most charming.

Jacques Grange

L'un des décorateurs les plus recherchés du monde, Jacques Grange ne passe pas autant de temps qu'il le souhaiterait dans sa ferme restaurée près de Saint-Rémy-de-Provence. C'est dommage car c'est une vraie maison: simple, confortable et pleine d'éléments originaux qui surprennent ou amusent sans jamais lasser. C'est une bâtisse provençale, décorée avec un sens de l'humour et du lieu, qui échappe à tous les clichés. Le jardin est à échelle humaine, rempli d'arbres fruitiers et de fleurs. Un banc a été placé de façon à admirer la vue. La maison regorge de chapeaux de paille, de paniers en osier provenant de la boutique du village et de piles de bouquins. Dans le garde-manger bien fourni, les pots de tapenade et de confiture faits maison avoisinent des piles d'assiettes en céramique colorées venant de la région. Il y a une grande cheminée où l'on fait cuire le dîner que l'on mange ensuite sur la table de la cuisine … Bref, c'est une maison où il fait bon vivre et même s'il ne s'agit pas du décor le plus grandiose de Jacques Grange, c'est certainement le plus charmant.

Als einer der gefragtesten Innenausstatter verbringt Jacques Grange weniger Zeit in seinem umgebauten Bauernhaus in der Nähe von Saint-Rémy-de-Provence, als ihm lieb wäre. Das ist sehr bedauerlich, denn es ist ein echtes Zuhause: einfach, gemütlich und voller wahrhaft inspirierender Stücke, die überraschen oder amüsieren, aber niemals überwältigen. Dieses provenzalische Haus wurde mit ebensoviel Sinn für Humor wie für Räumlichkeit ausgestattet. Der Garten voller Obstbäume und Blumen ist auf ein menschliches Maß zugeschnitten. Eine günstig plazierte Bank steht genau an der richtigen Stelle, damit man die Aussicht optimal genießen kann. Im Inneren gibt es reichlich Strohhüte, Weidenkörbe aus dem Dorfladen und Berge von Büchern. In der wohlgefüllten Speisekammer stehen hausgemachte Konfitüre und »tapenade« neben Stapeln ortstypischer bunter Keramik. Über dem offenen Feuer wird das Abendessen gegrillt, das man anschließend am Küchentisch serviert… Es ist wahrhaftig eine Freude, in diesem Haus zu leben, und wenn es vielleicht auch nicht Granges großartigstes Werk darstellt, so ist es doch sicher sein bezauberndstes.

Above: the lawn, left to run a little wild and spiked with aromatic herbs, and the ochre L-shaped façade of Mas Mireïo.
On the following pages: the Alpilles mountain range as seen from the garden.

Ci-dessus: la façade ocre en «L» du Mas Mireïo côté jardin, où les herbes folles sont parsemées de plantes aromatiques.
Double page suivante: la chaîne des Alpilles vue du jardin.

Oben: der ein bißchen verwilderte, mit duftenden Kräutern durchsetzte Rasen und die ockerfarbene L-Form der Fassade des Mas Mireïo.
Folgende Doppelseite: Blick vom Garten auf die Bergkette der Alpilles.

Above: *a view of the permanently cluttered library showing a selection of amusing curiosities.*
Facing page: *a table displaying ceramic vases and a drawing by Picasso.*
On the following pages: *a view of the living room, showing the forties' armchairs and an iron "toro de fuego" bought in Perpignan which observes the aspiring artists sitting at the wide oak table ready to draw the garden view.*
Pages 118/119: *a view into the kitchen.*

Ci-dessus: *la bibliothèque, avec son désordre savant d'objets drôles et inattendus.*
Page de droite: *une nature morte avec des vases en céramique et un dessin de Picasso.*
Double page suivante: *le salon, avec des fauteuils des années quarante. Le «toro de fuego» en fer acheté à Perpignan observe les aspirants artistes qui s'asseoient à la grande table en chêne pour croquer le jardin.*
Pages 118/119: *une vue de la cuisine.*

Oben: *ein Blick in die stets unordentliche Bibliothek mit einer Sammlung interessanter Kuriositäten.*
Rechte Seite: *ein Stilleben mit Keramikvasen und einer Zeichnung von Picasso.*
Folgende Doppelseite: *Blick ins Wohnzimmer mit Lehnstühlen aus den vierziger Jahren und einem eisernen »toro de fuego«, den Grange in Perpignan erwarb und der die Künstler in spe am großen Eichentisch beobachtet, wenn sie dabei sind, das Gartenpanorama zu zeichnen.*
Seiten 118/119: *ein Blick in die Küche.*

The fashion designer Michel Klein, who now designs the couture collection for Guy Laroche, is internationally recognized as a modernist, and his collections are often exercises in purity: monochromatic and sober. In marked contrast to his fashion work, he is a great believer in colour as an essential decorative element for interiors. In his Provençal retreat near Arles he has chosen a different, luminous tone for each room. With the enthusiasm of a child spoilt for choice before a box of finger paints, he daubed his restored "mas" in fuchsia, canary yellow, a vibrant red, emerald green and a blue-mauve that changes colour with the light. In fact he confesses that the most exciting moment in the whole project was choosing the colours from the rainbow of pigments available at Sennelier in Paris. This audacious mix has worked perfectly, opening up the low, vaulted spaces and bringing the incomparable Provençal springtime palette into the house: sunflowers, poppies, deep green cyprus trees and the shifting blues of the sky, are all reflected in the shades on the walls.

Michel Klein

Le styliste Michel Klein, qui dessine désormais les collections de haute couture de Guy Laroche, est reconnu partout dans le monde comme un moderniste dont les créations sobres et monochromes sont des exemples de pureté. En revanche, quand il s'agit de décorer sa maison, Klein croit en la couleur. Dans sa retraite provençale, près d'Arles, il a peint chaque pièce d'un ton différent, rivalisant de luminosité. Avec l'ivresse d'un enfant devant sa première boîte de couleurs, il a badigeonné les murs de fuchsia, de jaune canari, de rouge vif et de bleu vert qui changent de teintes au gré de la lumière. De fait, il avoue que la partie la plus excitante de la restauration de son mas a été de choisir les couleurs dans l'arc-en-ciel de pigments proposés par la boutique parisienne de Sennelier. Ce mélange audacieux a fait des miracles: toutes les couleurs du printemps provençal, tournesols, coquelicots, verts sombres des cyprès et bleus changeants du ciel se retrouvent sur les murs de la maison.

Der Modeschöpfer Michel Klein, der inzwischen die Kollektion für das Couture-Haus Guy Laroche entwirft, ist international als Modernist anerkannt. Seine monochromen, nüchternen Kollektionen sind oft Variationen von Schlichtheit. Im Gegensatz zu seinem Modeschaffen schätzt er jedoch bei Innenräumen starke Farben als dekoratives Element. In seinem provenzalischen Haus in der Nähe von Arles wählte er für jeden Raum einen anderen leuchtenden Farbton. Mit der Begeisterung eines Kindes, das aufgeregt vor einem Kasten mit Fingerfarben sitzt, entschied er sich bei der Renovierung seines »mas« für Fuchsie, Kanariengelb, Leuchtendrot, Smaragdgrün und ein Malvenblau, das sich je nach Lichteinfall verändert. Er gesteht sogar, der aufregendste Moment bei dem ganzen Projekt sei für ihn die Auswahl der Farben aus der Palette an Pigmenten gewesen, die bei Sennelier in Paris angeboten wurden. Die kühne Mischung hat sich optimal bewährt; sie macht die niedrigen, gewölbten Räume offener und bringt die einzigartige Palette der provenzalischen Frühlingsfarben ins Haus: Sonnenblumen, Mohn, tiefgrüne Zypressen und das changierende Blau des Himmels – all das spiegelt sich in den Wandfarben.

Above and right: the garden façade of the house with topiaries, aloes
and geraniums and a combination of antique garden furniture.
On the following pages: A "star" chandelier by Orn Gudmundarsen
lights a summer dinner table in the garden under the century-old
plane trees.

Ci-dessus et à droite: la façade côté jardin avec ses buissons, ses
aloès, ses géraniums et un ensemble de meubles de jardin anciens.
Double page suivante: un lustre «étoile» dessiné par Orn Gudmundarsen éclaire le dîner d'été sous les platanes centenaires.

Oben und rechts: Die Gartenseite des Hauses mit Formbäumen,
Aloe und Geranien sowie einer Ansammlung alter Gartenmöbel.
Folgende Doppelseite: Der Stern-Kerzenleuchter von Orn Gudmundarsen beleuchtet im Garten einen Sommer-Eßtisch unter jahrhundertealten Platanen.

Facing page: the main room with its ancient, vaulted ceiling. The decor is an eclectic mix of tribal sculpture, local pottery and 19th-century knick-knacks. The delicate, straight-backed chairs date from the Restoration.
Above: The red room boasts contrasting yellow beams. The sideboard is an 18th-century weaver's table in oak. The giant agave is in zinc and is reflected in a Regency gilt mirror.
On the following pages: a view of the living room.

Page de gauche: la pièce principale, avec son plafond voûté. Le décor est un mélange éclectique de sculptures primitives, de poteries de la région et de bibelots du XIXe siècle. Les délicates chaises à dos droit datent de la Restauration.
Ci-dessus: dans la chambre rouge, les poutres apparentes ont été peintes en jaune pour un effet de contraste. La console en chêne est une table de tisserand du XVIIIe siècle. L'agave géant en zinc se reflète dans un miroir Régence en bois doré.
Double page suivante: le salon.

Linke Seite: der Hauptraum mit seiner alten Gewölbedecke. Die Ausstattung ist eine eklektische Mixtur aus primitiven Plastiken, örtlichen Töpferwaren und Trödel aus dem 19. Jahrhundert. Die eleganten Stühle mit den geraden Lehnen stammen aus der Restaurationszeit.
Oben: das rote Zimmer mit stark kontrastierenden gelben Balken. Die Anrichte ist ein Webertisch aus Eiche aus dem 18. Jahrhundert. Die riesige Agave besteht aus Zink und wird von einem vergoldeten Régence-Spiegel reflektiert.
Folgende Doppelseite: Blick in das Wohnzimmer.

Facing page: *a bedroom with a bed which is an Empire "lit bateau". The red leatherette cupboard is a gypsy piece.*
Above: *a corridor which is an unabashed celebration of contrasting colours with the rooms. The white wrought-iron chairs are 1940s.*

Page de gauche: *une des chambres à coucher avec un lit bateau Empire et une commode de gitan en similicuir.*
Ci-dessus: *le couloir qui, avec les chambres, est un hymne à la couleur. Les chaises blanches en fer forgé datent des années quarante.*

Linke Seite: *ein Schlafzimmer. Das Bett ist ein »Lit bateau« aus der Empire-Zeit, das mit rotem Kunstleder überzogene Schränkchen eine Zigeunerarbeit.*
Oben: *Der Flur zeigt zusammen mit den Zimmern die unverhohlene Freude an Kontrastfarben. Die weißen schmiedeeisernen Stühle stammen aus den vierziger Jahren.*

Above: The wooden Louis XVI bed is upholstered in Colombian ticking, the armchairs are 18th century, and the painting on the right is by Jacquemond.
Facing page: a view into the lilac-blue bedroom from the corridor, showing a Napoleon III chair and a gilt Restoration mirror.

Ci-dessus: le lit en bois Louis XVI est tapissé de toile à matelas colombienne. Les fauteuils sont du XVIIIe siècle et le tableau sur la droite est signé Jacquemond.
Page de droite: la chambre bleu lilas vue du couloir, avec une chaise Napoléon III et un miroir Restauration en bois doré.

Oben: Das hölzerne Louis-XVI.-Bett ist mit kolumbianischem Matratzendrillich gepolstert, die Lehnstühle sind aus dem 18. Jahrhundert, das Gemälde rechts ist von Jacquemond.
Rechte Seite: Blick vom Flur in das blauviolette Schlafzimmer mit einem Napoleon-III-Stuhl und einem Spiegel aus der Restaurationszeit.

Unang, which owes its Germanic-sounding name to the Visigoth oc-
cupation of Provence, lies quietly, almost secretly nestled against the
hillside in the valley of the Nesque River. It is thought to be the oldest
chateau in the Vaucluse; indeed a thousand years have passed since
the first mention of the property was recorded, when Charles, King of
Provence, donated it to the church. For many hundreds of years an
important religious retreat, it is still flanked by the ancient private
chapel dedicated to Saint Gabriel. The main building's present ap-
pearance owes more to a certain Augustin Raymond who embellished
the exterior in the late 18th century and added the charming "jardin
à la Française" in clipped box. Run as a private vineyard by a brother
and sister team who occasionally rent out rooms, Unang slumbers,
forgotten by time, and gazes out over a still unspoilt wooded valley.

Château Unang

Unang, qui doit son nom aux consonances germaniques à l'occupation de la Provence par les Wisigoths, est niché tranquillement,
presque secrètement, dans les collines de la vallée du Nesque. On
le tient pour le plus vieux château du Vaucluse: en effet, il est déjà
mentionné dans des archives vieilles de mille ans, à l'occasion de
son don à l'Eglise par Charles, roi de Provence. Importante retraite
religieuse pendant de longs siècles, il est encore flanqué d'une ancienne chapelle privée dédiée à saint Gabriel. Le corps principal du
bâtiment doit surtout son aspect actuel à un certain Augustin Raymond, qui en a embelli les façades à la fin du XVIIIe siècle et a
ajouté un charmant jardin à la française en buis taillé. Aujourd'hui
domaine vinicole géré par un frère et une sœur qui y louent parfois
des chambres, Unang somnole, oublié par le temps, et contemple
la vallée boisée encore intacte qui s'étend à ses pieds.

Der germanisch anmutende Name Unang erinnert daran, daß die
Provence einst von den Westgoten besetzt war. Das Schloß liegt in ru-
higer, fast abgeschiedener Lage an die Hänge des Tals des Nesque ge-
schmiegt. Es gilt als das älteste Schloß des Vaucluse und wurde zum
ersten Mal vor tausend Jahren erwähnt, als der provenzalische König
Karl es der Kirche schenkte. Jahrhundertelang war Unang ein wichti-
ger religiöser Zufluchtsort, und noch heute grenzt das Schloß an eine
alte Kapelle, die dem Erzengel Gabriel geweiht ist. Das jetzige Er-
scheinungsbild des Hauptgebäudes ist im wesentlichen auf einen ge-
wissen Augustin Raymond zurückzuführen, der das Äußere gegen
Ende des 18. Jahrhunderts verschönerte und den bezaubernden fran-
zösischen Garten mit den präzise beschnittenen Buchsbaumfiguren
anlegte. Das Schloß wird heute von einem Geschwisterpaar als priva-
ter Weingarten und gelegentlich auch als Hotel genutzt, schlummert
jedoch ansonsten abseits vom Lauf der Zeit an seinem Aussichtspunkt
hoch über dem noch unverdorbenen, waldreichen Tal.

On the previous pages: *a view of the well-kept garden which surrounds the chateau.*
Above: *a corner of the beamed salon.*
Facing page: *a welcoming fire in the hall. Successive owners have transformed the classical proportions of a medieval chateau into a labyrinth of small rooms. Only a few original features remain, and Unang's interior documents the repeated changes in use common to many of the older Provençal chateaux. They were first transformed from feudal fortresses into monasteries, then into pleasure pavilions in the 18th century, and eventually into private homes or farms during the last century.*

Double page précédente: *le jardin très bien entretenu qui entoure le château.*
Ci-dessus: *le salon avec ses poutres apparentes.*
Page de droite: *un feu crépite chaleureusement dans le hall. Les différents propriétaires qui se sont succédés ont modifié les proportions classiques du château médiéval, devenu un dédale de petites pièces. Il reste peu des traits originaux d'Unang qui illustre les nom-*

breux changements de fonction subis par la plupart des vieux châteaux provençaux. Ces forteresses médiévales furent d'abord transformées en monastères, puis en pavillons de plaisance au XVIIIe siècle et enfin en maisons particulières ou en domaines agricoles au cours du siècle passé.

Vorhergehende Doppelseite: *Blick über den gepflegen Garten, der das Schloß umgibt.*
Oben: *eine Ecke des von einer Balkendecke überspannten Salons.*
Rechte Seite: *In der Halle lodert ein einladendes Kaminfeuer. Mehrere Besitzer haben nacheinander die klassischen Proportionen des mittelalterlichen Schlosses in ein Labyrinth kleiner Räume verwandelt. Von den Originalelementen blieben nur wenige erhalten. Die Innenausstattung zeugt von der immer wieder veränderten Nutzung, der viele der alten provenzalischen Châteaux sich unterwerfen mußten, die zunächst von feudalen Festungen in Klöster, im 18. Jahrhundert dann in Lustschlösser und im letzten Jahrhundert schließlich in private Wohnhäuser oder Gutshöfe umfunktioniert wurden.*

There are many ways of living in Provence: this small "mas", situated near Vaison-la-Romaine, has been restored in a completely original manner by the designer and decorator Denis Colomb. An "Aixerois" by birth, Colomb has a true understanding of the intimate character of his native Provence, and in accordance with his clients' wishes, he has avoided the conventions usually applied when decorating local holiday homes. The countryside in this mountainous area of the Vaucluse can be particularly wild and the plant growth invasive. Denis has preserved the garden much as the previous country tenant, a "paysan", left it and only slightly tamed the invading creepers that have almost swallowed the house. Inside he has kept the roughness of the walls, the uneven floor and the generally shabby-chic atmosphere of the place. Indeed, the traces of his intervention have been kept to a minimum. His client is thrilled as his interpretation is close to her conception of what modern-day country living is all about.

Denis Colomb

On peut vivre la Provence de multiples façons: ce petit mas situé près de Vaison-la-Romaine a été restauré avec une grande originalité par le décorateur et designer Denis Colomb. Aixois de naissance, Colomb a une profonde connaissance du caractère intime de sa Provence natale et, tout en respectant les souhaits de ses clients, il a évité les conventions qui caractérisent les maisons de vacances de la région. Le paysage de cette région montagneuse du Vaucluse est particulièrement sauvage et la végétation, envahissante. Denis a conservé le jardin pratiquement tel que l'avait laissé son ancien propriétaire, un agriculteur, se contentant d'apprivoiser les plantes grimpantes qui avaient pratiquement englouti la maison. A l'intérieur, il a préservé la texture brute des murs, le sol irrégulier et l'atmosphère générale d'élégant délabrement. De fait, son intervention est restée minime. Sa cliente est aux anges, car son intérieur correspond exactement à l'idée qu'elle se faisait de la vie moderne à la campagne.

Man kann auf ganz unterschiedliche Weise in der Provence wohnen. Dieser kleine »mas« in der Nähe von Vaison-la-Romaine wurde vom Designer und Innenausstatter Denis Colomb vollkommen originalgetreu renoviert. Colomb wurde in Aix geboren und hat schon von daher viel Sinn für den geheimen Charakter seiner provenzalischen Heimat. Im Einklang mit den Wünschen seiner Kunden läßt er bei der Renovierung von Ferienhäusern die üblichen Konventionen außer acht. Die Landschaft in diesem gebirgigen Teil des Vaucluse ist zum Teil recht wild, und die Vegetation überwuchert fast alles. Denis bewahrte den Garten im wesentlichen so, wie ihn der Vorbesitzer, ein Bauer, hinterließ, und stutzte lediglich die enormen Kletterpflanzen, die das Haus fast zu verschlingen drohten. Im Innern behielt er die rauhen Wände, den unebenen Fußboden und die insgesamt schäbig-schicke Atmosphäre des Hauses im großen und ganzen bei und verwischte die Spuren seiner Eingriffe, so gut es ging. Seine Kundin ist begeistert von seiner Konzeption, die ihren eigenen Vorstellungen von einem modernen Landleben entspricht.

Above: The multicoloured picket gate, shown in the detail on the left page, sets the stage for the vibrant walled courtyard, painted a deep Indian pink.
Right: the stone guesthouse in the garden, built with the renowned local technique of drystone walling, so distinctive an element in the indigenous architecture.

Ci-dessus: la clôture en piquets multicolores, montrée par le détail à la page de gauche, donne le ton de la cour, peinte d'un rose indien vibrant.
A droite: la maison d'amis dans le jardin, construite en «pierre sèche», une technique locale qui donne leur aspect si particulier aux paysages de la région.

Oben: Das auf der linken Seite abgebildete bunte Gartentor kündigt den dynamisch wirkenden, ummauerten Innenhof an, der in intensivem Indischrot gestrichen ist.
Rechts: das steinerne Gästehaus im Garten. Es wurde in der berühmten Trockenmauertechnik errichtet, die ein unverwechselbares Element der hiesigen Architektur darstellt.

Provence Interiors   Denis Colomb

Facing page: a corner of the master bedroom in the high-roofed converted hayloft. The mistress of the house has a penchant for old army jackets, some of which are displayed. The curtains have been magicked up out of Indian sugar sacks.
Above: a corner of the beamed living room, showing the rustic dining-table and an assortment of odd chairs.

Page de gauche: un angle de la chambre de maître sous le haut plafond de l'ancien fenil. La maîtresse de maison a un petit faible pour les vieilles vestes militaires, dont on peut voir ici quelques spécimens. Les rideaux ont été taillés dans des sacs à sucre indiens.
Ci-dessus: un coin du salon, avec ses poutres apparentes, une table rustique et un assortiment de chaises dépareillées.

Linke Seite: ein Winkel im Schlafzimmer unter dem hohen Dach des umgebauten Heubodens. Die Hausherrin hat eine Schwäche für abgetragene Armeejacken, von denen einige hier aushängen. Die Vorhänge wurden aus indischen Zuckersäcken gezaubert.
Oben: eine Ecke des Wohnzimmers mit seiner Balkendecke, dem rustikalen Eßtisch und einer Sammlung von Einzelstühlen.

Above and facing page: *two views of the kitchen, which pays homage to the art of non-designer decorating. The colourful clutter includes numerous bits and pieces picked up at local "brocantes", and souvenirs of frequent trips to Morocco and India.*

Ci-dessus et page de droite: *la cuisine, un hommage à l'art de décorer sans en avoir l'air. Le bric-à-brac coloré est fait de nombreux objets glanés dans les brocantes locales et de souvenirs de fréquents séjours au Maroc et en Inde.*

Oben und rechte Seite: *zwei Ansichten der Küche, die eine klare Absage an Designer-Einrichtungen darstellt. Das kunterbunte Durcheinander umfaßt zahlreiche Nippesteile, die bei örtlichen «brocantes» aufgestöbert wurden, sowie Souvenirs von vielen Reisen nach Marokko und Indien.*

Xavier Nicod is a bright, young, good-looking antique dealer based in L'Isle-sur-la-Sorgue. He has exceptionally sophisticated tastes and an address book of past clients that reads like "Celebrity News". Xavier Nicod has brought a breath of fresh air to the world of Provençal decorating. He's the man to see for a draper's table, pharmacist's chest of drawers, a roll-top desk from a provincial accountant's office or a set of 18th-century garden furniture rusted to just the right degree. He has a fine eye, and his liking for light, simple pieces is very much in tune with contemporary taste. He did not discover his vocation, however, until he bought a ruined village house in Goult when he was twenty. He did a lot of the rebuilding himself, on the advice of his great friend Bruno Brunello. When it came to the decorating, he began to scour the surrounding countryside with a passion that, quite naturally, revealed his true vocation. As soon as the house was furnished, he opened his shop – to sell off the surplus!

Xavier Nicod

Jeune, talentueux, et séduisant, Xavier Nicod, antiquaire, habite à L'Isle-sur-la-Sorgue. Il a un goût exceptionnel et un carnet d'adresse d'anciens clients digne du who's who du show-business. Xavier Nicod a apporté une bouffée d'air frais à la décoration provençale. C'est l'homme qui vous trouve la table de drapier, la commode de pharmacien, le secrétaire à cylindre de clerc de notaire ou l'ensemble de meubles de jardin XVIIIème rouillé juste ce qu'il faut. Il a un œil aiguisé et une préférence pour les pièces légères et sobres, parfaitement en harmonie avec le goût contemporain. Il n'a découvert sa vocation que vers l'âge de vingt ans, après avoir acheté une vieille maison de village en ruines à Goult. Il a effectué lui-même une bonne partie des travaux, sur les conseils de son grand ami Bruno Brunello. Le moment venu de s'attaquer à la décoration, il s'est mis à battre la campagne environnante avec un enthousiasme qui, très naturellement, lui a révélé sa vraie passion. Sitôt sa maison meublée, il a ouvert une boutique pour revendre le surplus!

Xavier Nicod ist ein intelligenter, gutaussehender junger Antiquitätenhändler mit Sitz in L'Isle-sur-la-Sorgue. Er besitzt einen exquisiten Geschmack und ein Adressbuch voller Kunden, das sich wie ein »Who is Who« der feinen Welt liest. Xavier Nicod brachte frischen Wind in die Welt der provenzalischen Innenarchitektur. Ihn schaltet man ein, wenn man einen Apothekerschrank, einen Rolladenschreibtisch aus einem provinziellen Buchhalterbüro oder einen Satz Gartenmöbel aus dem 18. Jahrhundert sucht. Er hat ein scharfes Auge und liegt mit seiner Vorliebe für helle, schlichte Stücke genau im Trend der Zeit. Dabei erkannte er seine Berufung erst, als er zwanzig war. Damals kaufte er ein verfallenes Häuschen in Goult. Einen großen Teil der Renovierungsarbeiten erledigte er selbst unter der Anleitung seines guten Freundes Bruno Brunello. Als es dann um die Innenausstattung ging, begann er die Umgebung mit einer Begeisterung durchzukämmen, die ihm auf ganz natürliche Art und Weise seine eigentliche Bestimmung deutlich machte. Kaum war sein Haus fertig eingerichtet, eröffnete er sein Geschäft – um den Überschuß zu verkaufen!

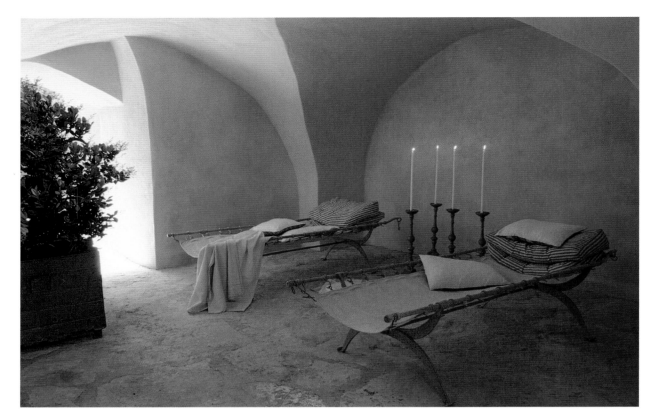

Previous pages: *views of the garden and a detail of the outdoor shower adjacent to the master bedroom that Nicod calls "a paradisaical experience" and uses even in the winter, a season which tends to be fairly mild in the region.*
Above: *a favourite spot for a siesta in the vaulted cellar that used to be the stable and which stays cool throughout the summer. The campbeds are 19th century.*
Facing page: *the dining-room, where the plaster has been mixed with Roussillon ochre to obtain the saffron tint on the walls. The massive table is a piece of "art populaire", made by fishermen for their cottages near Marseille. The candlesticks are fifties, the garden chairs are early 20th century. The embroidered straw carpet is Moroccan.*
Following pages: *Nicod's bedroom, with 19th-century rounded bedside tables, and his daughter Beryl's room, with an original 19th-century canopied fourposter bed. Both rooms are painted a refreshing sea green.*

Pages précédentes: *le jardin et un détail de la douche extérieure attenante à la chambre de maître. Nicod la qualifie «d'expérience paradisiaque» et l'utilise même en hiver, saison relativement douce dans cette région.*
Ci-dessus: *le coin idéal pour la sieste, dans la cave voûtée qui servait autrefois d'écurie et qui reste fraîche tout l'été. Les lits de camp datent du XIXe siècle.*
Page de droite: *la salle à manger. L'enduit au plâtre a été mélangé avec de l'ocre du Roussillon pour obtenir la teinte safran des murs. La table massive est une pièce d'art populaire, construite par des*

pêcheurs pour leur cabanon près de Marseille. Les bougeoirs datent des années cinquante et les chaises, du début du siècle. Le tapis en paille brodé est marocain.
Pages suivantes: *la chambre de Xavier Nicod avec ses tables de chevet arrondies dix-neuvième; la chambre de sa fille Beryl, avec un lit à baldaquin du dix-neuvième. Les deux chambres sont peintes d'une rafraîchissante couleur vert d'eau.*

Vorhergehende Seiten: *Ansichten des Gartens und Detail einer Dusche im Freien neben dem Schlafzimmer – eine Einrichtung, die Nicod eine »paradiesische Erfahrung« nennt und die er sogar im Winter nutzt, der in dieser Gegend allerdings recht mild ist.*
Oben: *Ein idealer Ort für eine Siesta ist der Gewölbekeller, der früher ein Stall war und auch im Sommer schön kühl bleibt. Die Feldbetten stammen aus dem 19. Jahrhundert.*
Rechte Seite: *das Eßzimmer, für das der Putz direkt mit dem Ocker aus Roussilllon angemischt wurde, um den warmen Safranton der Wände zu erzielen. Der massive Tisch ist ein Stück volkstümliches Kunsthandwerk, das von Fischern für ihre Hütten in der Nähe von Marseille angefertigt wurde. Die Kerzenhalter stammen aus den fünfziger Jahren, die Gartenstühle vom Beginn des 20. Jahrhunderts. Der bestickte Strohteppich ist eine marokkanische Arbeit.*
Folgende Seiten: *Xavier Nicods Schlafzimmer mit abgerundeten Nachttischen aus dem 19. Jahrhundert und das Zimmer seiner Tochter Beryl mit einem echten Baldachinbett aus dem 19. Jahrhundert. Beide Räume sind in angenehm kühlem Wassergrün gestrichen.*

Provence Interiors   Xavier Nicod

This village house, perched high above the plain and sheltered by the Lubéron mountains, is an imposing 16th and 17th-century construction. The Mayers bought it many years ago from a military gentleman whose family had lived in the house for several generations. Tony Mayer, author of a book on "La Vie Anglaise", considers himself something of an Anglophile and is greatly amused by the hordes of English tourists who have taken to invading the quiet hilltop village during the summer months. Owing to the Mayers' advanced age, the house has remained untouched for the last twenty years and thus could be considered a rare example of a well-preserved interior in a style that has almost vanished. Many comparable gracious Provençal properties have been bought up by a new generation of aesthetes and been transformed.

Marie-Thérèse et Tony Mayer

Cette imposante bâtisse des XVIe et XVIIe siècles est située dans un village haut perché au-dessus de la plaine et abrité par les montagnes du Lubéron. Les Mayer l'ont achetée il y a de nombreuses années à un militaire dont la famille y vivait depuis plusieurs générations. Anglophile averti, Tony Mayer, auteur de «La vie anglaise», est très amusé par les nuées de touristes britanniques qui s'abattent sur la colline tranquille pendant les mois d'été. Du fait de l'âge avancé des Mayer, la maison n'a pas changé depuis vingt ans et constitue donc un exemple rare d'un style de décor comme on n'en voit plus. De nombreuses belles demeures provençales ont été rachetées depuis par une nouvelle génération d'esthètes qui ont imposé d'autres concepts de la décoration intérieure.

Das hoch über der Ebene im Schatten des Lubéron-Gebirges liegende Haus ist ein eindrucksvolles Gebäude aus dem 16. und 17. Jahrhundert. Die Mayers kauften es vor vielen Jahren einem Offizier ab, dessen Familie es mehrere Generationen lang bewohnt hatte. Tony Mayer, Autor eines Buches über »La Vie Anglaise«, hält sich selbst für ausgeprägt anglophil und amüsiert sich königlich über die Horden englischer Touristen, die in den Sommermonaten in das stille Bergdörfchen einfallen. Aufgrund des hohen Alters des Ehepaares ist an dem Haus in den letzten zwanzig Jahren nichts mehr verändert worden. Es besitzt daher eine gut erhaltene Innenausstattung in einem eigentlich nicht mehr üblichen Stil. Viele ähnlich schöne Besitzungen in der Provence sind mittlerweile von einer jungen Generation von Liebhabern aufgekauft und umgestaltet worden.

On the previous pages: *the view from the disused well in the garden, previously the only source of water in the house.*
Below: *the library, a witness to Tony Mayer's literary activities. In their youth, the Mayers belonged to a highly artistic circle and frequently visited personalities such as Cocteau and Picabia, both of whose drawings and other mementos are present in the room. In the foreground, rustic Provençal chairs and a solid, traditional dining-table now used as a desk.*

Double page précédente: *la vue depuis le puits condamné du jardin, autrefois la seule source d'eau de la maison.*
Ci-dessous: *la bibliothèque, siège des activités littéraires de Tony Mayer. Dans leur jeunesse, les Mayer faisaient partie de l'élite artistique et fréquentaient des personnalités telles que Cocteau et Picabia, dont des dessins et autres souvenirs ornent cette pièce. Au premier plan, des chaises rustiques provençales et une lourde table de salle à manger traditionnelle reconvertie en bureau.*

Vorhergehende Doppelseite: *der Blick in den Garten von dem stillgelegten Brunnen aus, der früher die einzige Wasserquelle des Hauses war.*
Unten: *Die Bibliothek bezeugt Tony Mayers reges literarisches Interesse. In ihrer Jugend waren die Mayers in bedeutenden Künstlerkreisen zu Hause und hatten Kontakt zu Persönlichkeiten wie Cocteau und Picabia, deren Zeichnungen und andere Werke im Raum zu sehen sind. Im Vordergrund rustikale provenzalische Stühle und ein solider altehrwürdiger Eßtisch, der heute als Schreibtisch dient.*

Above: The original 16th-century fireplace is the focal point of the
long, low-beamed room. The ceiling has been painted white in order
to give the room a greater volume. In the foreground, an 18th-century
cane-bottomed bench, known as a "radassié", which is typically
Provençal.
On the following pages: the "salon d'été" in what used to be the
barn. The art nouveau pieces are by Jacques Majorelle.

Ci-dessus: Cette longue pièce au plafond bas et aux poutres apparentes est dominée par la cheminée d'origine qui date du XVIe siècle.
Le plafond a été peint en blanc pour agrandir le volume. Au premier
plan, un banc canné typiquement provençal, ou «radassié», qui date
du XVIIIe siècle.
Double page suivante: le salon d'été dans l'ancienne grange. Les
meubles Art nouveau sont de Jacques Majorelle.

Oben: Der originalgetreue Kamin aus dem 16. Jahrhundert ist
das Herz des langgestreckten Raumes. Die niedrige Balkendecke
wurde weiß gestrichen, um den Raum größer wirken zu lassen.
Im Vordergrund eine typisch provenzalische Bank mit einer aus
Schilf geflochtenen Sitzfläche, »Radassié« genannt.
Folgende Doppelseite: der »Salon d'été«, das Wohnzimmer für den
Sommer, in der ehemaligen Scheune. Die Jugendstilstücke stammen
von Jacques Majorelle.

Provence Interiors   Anna Bonde et Arne Tengblad

The Swedish painter Arne Tengblad discovered the Lubéron in 1963, while visiting a painter friend. He bought his first ruin for next to nothing, and with Anna Bonde decided to move to Provence for good. They have since bought and restored several houses: once they have made them comfortable, they tend to get the urge to move on and start again. Indeed, this partly troglodytic village house is their sixth. The house assumed its present appearance in the 1680s when a village girl was married off to the Spanish court of Asturias. While cleaning out the cellar Tengblad discovered a 12th-century coat of arms, proof of the building's mysterious past. Together the couple have tried to restore some of the original gracious feeling of space and have created an unexpected loft-like area for their main room. The house is decorated with market finds and fine pieces of Swedish furniture for which Anna designs the upholstery fabric.

Anna Bonde et Arne Tengblad

Le peintre suédois Arne Tengblad a découvert le Lubéron en 1963 en rendant visite à un ami peintre. Il y a acheté sa première ruine pour une bouchée de pain et, avec Anna Bonde, a décidé de s'établir définitivement en Provence. Depuis, ils ont acheté et restauré plusieurs maisons: chaque fois, après les avoir rendues confortables, ils ont été pris d'une envie de déménager et de repartir à zéro. Cette maison de village en partie troglodyte est leur sixième. Elle n'a revêtu son aspect actuel que vers 1680, lorsqu'une jeune fille du village fut mariée à un ambassadeur de la cour du prince des Asturies. En nettoyant la cave, Tengblad a toutefois découvert aussi un blason du XIIe siècle, preuve du passé mystérieux de l'édifice. Le couple a tenté de retrouver certains des élégants volumes d'origine et a créé un espace inattendu de type loft qui leur sert de pièce principale. La maison est décorée de trouvailles dénichées sur le marché local et de beaux meubles suédois pour lesquels Anna dessine des tissus.

Der schwedische Maler Arne Tengblad lernte den Lubéron 1963 kennen, als er dort einen befreundeten Maler besuchte. Seine erste Ruine bekam er fast geschenkt, worauf er beschloß, zusammen mit Anna Bonde für immer in die Provence zu ziehen. Seither haben die beiden mehrere Häuser gekauft und restauriert. Sobald sie ein Haus fertig eingerichtet haben, drängt es sie schon, mit dem nächsten wieder von vorne zu beginnen. Das hier abgebildete Haus, das zum Teil wie eine Höhle wirkt, ist ihr sechstes. Das Gebäude erhielt sein heutiges Aussehen in den achtziger Jahren des 17. Jahrhunderts, als ein Mädchen einen Gesandten vom Hofe des Prinzen von Asturien heiratete. Beim Entrümpeln des Kellers fand Tengblad auch ein Wappen aus dem 12. Jahrhundert, das von der geheimnisvollen Geschichte des Hauses zeugt. Gemeinsam bemühte sich das Paar, einige der noch originalen schönen Räume zu restaurieren, und richtete eine ungewöhnliche, dachhohe Halle als Hauptraum ein. Die Einrichtung besteht aus Zufallsfunden und aparten schwedischen Antiquitäten, für die Anna selbst die Polsterstoffe entwirft.

Above: A school teaching aid picturing a zebra hangs above a simple
day bed in wrought iron designed by Anna. The iron chair was found
in a market.
Detail right: a Swedish chair and a baroque Italian 17th-century
chandelier.
Facing page: The main room houses a collection of contemporary
art.

Ci-dessus: une planche d'école représentant un zèbre est suspendue
au-dessus d'un simple lit de repos en fer forgé dessiné par Anna. La
chaise en métal a été trouvée sur le marché.
Détail de droite: une chaise suédoise et un lustre baroque italien du
XVIIe siècle.
Page de droite: la collection d'art contemporain dans la pièce
principale.

Oben: Ein Schulhilfsmittel mit einem Zebra hängt über einer von
Anna selbst entworfenen, schlichten schmiedeeisernen Liege. Der
Eisenstuhl wurde auf einem Markt entdeckt.
Detail rechts: ein schwedischer Sessel und ein barocker italienischen
Kerzenleuchter aus dem 17. Jahrhundert.
Rechte Seite: Der Hauptraum beherbergt eine Sammlung moderner
Kunst.

Niched deep in the stone of a hilltop village in the Lubéron, Nicole de Vesian's home is a completely original creation. As soon as you step through the door, the intoxicating smell of lavender leaves you light-headed. Underfoot, in the entrance, are loose, large pebbles, known as "galets", from the nearby river, the Durance. The house, issue of the stone itself, was converted from two ruined cottages and the covered lane that ran between them. Three steps up to the guest room, three steps down to the lounge, it is oddly distributed and betrays its unusual origins. Everywhere the monochromatic beige, cream and off-white, beloved of Nicole, allow the strong contours of the stone to impose a very particular atmosphere. The difference between the garden and its pebbled paths and the stone-walled interior with its bouquets of dried flowers and budding plants seems minimal.

Nicole de Vesian

Profondément nichée dans la pierre d'un village haut perché du Lubéron, la maison de Nicole de Vesian est une création très originale. Dès que l'on passe la porte, on est saisi par le parfum enivrant de la lavande. Le sol du vestibule est pavé de gros galets qui proviennent de la Durance voisine. La maison, née de la pierre elle-même, a été construite en réunissant deux bâtisses en ruines et l'allée couverte qui les reliait. On monte trois marches pour accéder à la chambre d'amis, on en descend trois pour se rendre au salon: la distribution déroutante des pièces témoigne des origines inhabituelles de la maison. Partout, les tons monochromes de beige, de crème et de blanc cassé, chers à Nicole, laissent la pierre nue imposer une atmosphère très particulière. Entre le jardin et ses allées de gravier, et l'intérieur avec ses murs en pierres brutes, ses bouquets de fleurs séchées et ses plantes vertes, la frontière est ténue.

Tief in den Fels eines Bergdorfes im Lubéron gegraben liegt Nicole de Vesians ausgesprochen originelles Haus. Sobald man durch die Tür tritt, steigt einem der berauschende Lavendelduft zu Kopfe. Der Fußbodenbelag im Eingangsgereich besteht aus großen, losen Kieselsteinen, »galets«, die vom Ufer der nahe gelegenen Durance stammen. Das Haus ist teils direkt in den Fels hineingebaut, teils aus zwei verfallenen Bauernhäusern und dem überdachten Pfad zwischen ihnen zusammengesetzt. Drei Stufen führen hinauf zum Gästezimmer, drei Stufen hinab zum Wohnzimmer – mit seiner eigenwilligen Aufteilung verrät das Haus seine besonderen Ursprünge. Die von Nicole geliebten, monochrom eingesetzten Töne Beige, Creme und gebrochen Weiß, die die kraftvollen Konturen des Steins unterstreichen, verleihen dem Anwesen eine ganz eigentümliche Atmosphäre. Zwischen dem Garten mit seinem Kiesweg und den Innenräumen mit den Steinwänden, Trockenblumensträußen und üppigen Topfpflanzen besteht nur ein minimaler Unterschied.

On the previous pages: a view of Nicole de Vesian's innovative garden that has been a source of inspiration for many. By concentrating on hardy local varieties, as opposed to more showy imported plants, she has refined the concept of the Provençal garden. A hundred shades of green and grey, the indigenous aromatics clipped into spheres, and the proud and long-living trees of the area give a distinction and strange beauty to Nicole's terraced "terrain". Her creation is not about superfluous decoration, or about flowers even, but about form, and echoing the true shapes and colours of the region.
On these pages: the simple kitchen which makes a virtue of its clean lines and functional wooden furnishings.
On the following pages: the salon.

Double page précédente: le jardin de Nicole de Vesian dont beaucoup se sont inspirés. En préférant les variétés robustes de la région aux plantes plus spectaculaires venues d'ailleurs, elle a affiné le concept du jardin provençal. Une palette très nuancée de verts et de gris, des plantes aromatiques locales taillées en boules et les vieux arbres fiers de la région donnent à ce terrain en terrasse une distinction et une beauté étrange. Nicole de Vesian ne s'embarrasse pas de détails décoratifs superflus, ni même de fleurs, mais se concentre avant tout sur une vision d'ensemble qui rappelle les vraies formes et couleurs de la région.
Page de gauche et ci-dessus: le décor simple de la cuisine qui met en valeur ses lignes sobres et ses meubles en bois fonctionnels.
Double page suivante: le salon.

Vorhergehende Doppelseite: Ansichten von Nicoles innovativem Garten, der einen starken Einfluß auf andere Anlagen ausgeübt hat. Durch die Konzentration auf widerstandsfähige regionale Gewächse anstelle spektakulärer, importierter Pflanzen verfeinerte Nicole das Konzept des provenzalischen Gartens. Grün und Grau in Hunderten von Nuancen, zu Kugeln geschnittene einheimische Aromaten und die stolzen, langlebigen Bäume der Region verleihen dem terrassenförmig angelegten Garten eine ganz eigene, fremdartige Schönheit. Ihr geht es nicht um überflüssige Dekors, nicht einmal um Blumen, sondern allein um Formen. Der Garten spiegelt die Konturen und Farben, die in dieser Region tatsächlich zu finden sind.
Diese Doppelseite: Die schlichte Küche profitiert optisch von klaren Linien und funktionalen Holzmöbeln.
Folgende Doppelseite: der Salon.

Above and facing page: the bathroom and a little stone sink for rinsing one's hands.
On the following pages: the partly troglodytic summer dining-room which gives onto the garden through big double doors. Nicole's favourite room, it overflows with glorious clutter: garden utensils, straw hats and baskets, cuttings being carefully nurtured, garden furniture and dried flowers.

Ci-dessus et page de droite: la salle de bains et un petit lavabo en pierre pour se laver les mains.
Double page suivante: la salle à manger d'été à demi-creusée dans la roche donne sur le jardin à travers deux grandes double portes. Pièce préférée de Nicole, elle regorge d'un pittoresque bric-à-brac: outils de jardinage, chapeaux de paille, paniers en osier, boutures soigneusement nourries, meubles de jardin et fleurs séchées.

Oben und rechte Seite: das Badezimmer und ein kleines steinernes Becken zum Händewaschen.
Folgende Doppelseite: die teilweise höhlenartige Sommerküche, deren große Flügeltür zum Garten hinausgeht. Nicoles Lieblingsraum enthält ein prachtvolles Sammelsurium von Gartengeräten, Strohhüten und Körben, liebevoll gezogenen Ablegern, Gartenmöbeln und Trockenblumen.

Built on the site of a Celtic "oppidum", the Château d'Ansouis, ancient fief and ancestral home of the Sabran-Pontevès family, towers over the pretty stone Provençal village of the same name. Partly open to the public but still the family home of the Vicomte de Sabran-Pontevès, his wife and their four children, it gives an excellent idea of what a grand house is really like to live in. However unlikely it may seem, this huge rabbit warren of a house really has managed to conserve a cosy atmosphere. This could be due to the fact that, apart from a short period after the Revolution, members of the Sabran family have been living here for the last seven hundred years. Originally a 12th and 14th-century fortress, Ansouis was beautified in the 17th century. This later addition represents the main body of the chateau.

Château d'Ansouis

Bâti sur le site d'une ancienne citadelle celte, le Château d'Ansouis, autrefois fief et demeure de la famille Sabran-Pontevès, surplombe le ravissant village provençal du même nom. Partiellement ouvert au public, il est toujours habité par le vicomte de Sabran-Pontevès, sa femme et leurs quatre enfants, ce qui donne aux visiteurs une excellente idée de ce que signifie «la vie de château». Contre toute attente, une atmosphère douillette baigne ce gigantesque dédale de pièces et de couloirs. Cela s'explique sans doute par le fait qu'à l'exception d'une brève période après la Révolution, des membres de la famille Sabran y vivent depuis sept siècles. A l'origine forteresse des XIIe et XIVe siècles, le corps principal du château a été rénové et embelli au XVIIe.

Das über einem keltischen »oppidum« erbaute Schloß Ansouis, früheres Lehen und Wohnsitz der Familie Sabran-Pontevès, blickt auf das hübsche provenzalische Dorf gleichen Namens hinab. Das Schloß, in dem noch heute der Vicomte de Sabran-Pontevès mit seiner Frau und seinen vier Kindern lebt und das teilweise zur Besichtigung freigegeben ist, gibt einen vorzüglichen Eindruck davon, was es bedeutet, in einem echten Herrenhaus zu wohnen. Und so unwahrscheinlich es auch klingen mag, dieses Schloß, das aus einem ungeheuren Wirrwarr verschachtelter Räume besteht, hat sich eine gemütliche Atmosphäre bewahrt. Vielleicht liegt es daran, daß Mitglieder der Familie Sabran mit nur einer kurzen Unterbrechung nach der französischen Revolution seit siebenhundert Jahren hier leben. Das im 12. und 14. Jahrhundert ursprünglich als Festung angelegte Schloß wurde im 17. Jahrhundert umgebaut. Der jüngere, regelmäßigere Bauteil stellt heute das Hauptgebäude der Anlage dar.

Page 174: *a view of the splendid avenue of cypresses that lead off from the main gate. The famous hanging gardens at Ansouis include a topiary maze in clipped box, and the view from the terraces of the rolling Provençal counryside is quite breathtaking, as can be seen on the previous pages.*

Above: *one of the historical 17th-century bedrooms. Many of these are furnished with family heirlooms inherited from "tante" Huberte and "tante" Gersende, who were, respectively, the last Marquise of Sabran-Pontevès and the Marquise des Isnards.*

Facing page: *the games room in the private apartments of the present lady of the house, with its fancy plasterwork and pistacho paintwork.*

On the following pages: *the vaulted kitchen, one of the oldest rooms in the chateau, that dates from the times of the popular Provençal Saints Elzéar and Delphine de Sabran, whose lives were played out in the corridors of Ansouis.*

Page 174: *la majestueuse allée de cyprès qui mène au château. Les fameux jardins suspendus d'Ansouis comprennent un labyrinthe en buis taillés. Depuis les terrasses, on a une vue à couper le souffle sur les douces collines provençales, comme on peut le constater sur la double page précédente.*

Ci-dessus: *l'une des chambres historiques, avec son décor du XVIIe siècle. La plupart contiennent des meubles de famille hérités de «tante» Huberte et «tante» Gersende qui furent respectivement, la dernière marquise de Sabran-Pontevès et la marquise des Isnards.*

Page de droite: *la salle de jeu des appartements privés de la maîtresse de maison, avec ses murs pistache et ses «pâtisseries».*

Double page suivante: *la cuisine voûtée, l'une des pièces les plus anciennes du château. Elle remonte aux temps d'Elzéar et de Delphine de Sabran, deux saints provençaux très populaires qui vécurent à Ansouis.*

Page 174: *ein Blick in die prachtvolle Zypressenallee, die vom Haupttor zum Haus führt. Zu den berühmten hängenden Gärten von Ansouis gehört ein Labyrinth aus kunstvoll beschnittenem Buchsbaum. Die Aussicht von den Terrassen auf die provenzalische Hügellandschaft ist einzigartig, wie die vorhergehende Doppelseite beweist.*

Oben: *eines der originalgetreuen Schlafzimmer aus dem 17. Jahrhundert. Viele davon sind mit Möbeln aus Familienbesitz eingerichtet, Erbstücke von »Tante« Huberte, der letzten Marquise de Sabran-Pontevès, und »Tante« Gersende, der Marquise des Isnards.*

Rechte Seite: *Zu den Privatgemächern der jetzigen Hausherrin gehört dieser Salon mit seinen »Pâtisseries« aus Stuck und den pistaziengrün gestrichenen Wänden.*

Folgende Doppelseite: *Die mit einer Gewölbedecke ausgestattete Küche ist einer der ältesten Räume des Schlosses und stammt noch aus der Epoche der bis heute verehrten provenzalischen Heiligen Elzéar und Delphine de Sabran, die hier in Ansouis lebten und wirkten.*

A country house near Apt: It was the desert aspect of the harsh Provençal landscape lying beneath the contemporary view of the region as an earthly paradise that appealed to this sculptor, landscape gardener and professor of fine arts who has a passion for deserts. This was the inspiration behind his subtle design for the restoration of a ruined "bastide", a Provençal countryhouse. His home is monochromatic, organic and minimalist in a warm, earthy sort of way. With an American colleague from Chicago, influenced by the legacy of Mies van der Rohe, he simplified the units, coated the walls in limewash and sand from the local river and even designed his own furniture to give an overall impression of purity. The finished result is a celebration of the uncluttered lines of the rural stone architecture of the Provençal countryside. The landscape, the blonde stone and the flat façades of the "bastide" are echoed in the muted tones and textured walls of the house; a serene sculpture in an untamed environment.

Une bastide près d'Apt

C'est le paysage âpre et désertique de la Provence, la face cachée du «paradis terrestre» que l'on tend à y voir aujourd'hui, qui a séduit ce sculpteur, paysagiste, professeur de beaux-arts et passionné des déserts et l'a inspiré à restaurer avec raffinement une bastide en ruines. L'intérieur est monochrome, organique et minimaliste, mais dégage une atmosphère chaleureuse et terrienne. Avec un collègue américain de Chicago influencé par le travail de Mies van der Rohe, il a simplifié les volumes, enduit les murs de chaux et de sable provenant de la rivière voisine et conçu lui-même ses meubles afin de créer une impression générale de pureté. Le résultat est un hymne à l'architecture provençale. Le paysage, la pierre blonde et les façades plates des bastides se prolongent dans les tons étouffés et la texture travaillée des murs de la maison: sculpture sereine dans un environnement sauvage.

Ein Landhäuschen in der Nähe von Apt: Die wüstenhaften Elemente der herben provenzalischen Landschaft, die unter ihrem heutigen Image als Paradies auf Erden schlummern, sprachen den Bildhauer, Landschaftsgärtner und Kunstprofessor an, dessen besonderes Interesse Wüstenlandschaften gilt. Diese Vorliebe bewog ihn zu dem subtilen Design bei der Restaurierung einer verfallenen »bastide«. Sein Haus ist monochrom, organisch und auf eine warme, erdhafte Weise minimalistisch. Zusammen mit einem Kollegen, einem von Mies van der Rohe beeinflußten Amerikaner aus Chicago, vereinfachte er die Raumaufteilung, überzog die Wände mit Kalkfarbe und Sand aus dem nahe gelegenen Fluß und entwarf sogar die Möbel selbst, um den Eindruck umfassender Reinheit zu schaffen. Das Ergebnis ist ein Loblied auf die schnörkellosen Linien der bäuerlichen Steinarchitektur in der ländlichen Provence. Die Landschaft, der hellgelbe Stein und die glatten Fassaden der »bastide« werden in der gedämpften Farbgebung und den angerauhten Wänden des Hauses aufgenommen: eine heitere Skulptur in einer ungezähmten Umgebung.

Above: the simple lines of the 17-metre long swimming pool, built in stone from the nearby mountain village of Ménerbes. Sturdy, drought-resistant herbs such as rosemary and thyme are clipped into topiaries, as is evergreen honeysuckle.

Ci-dessus: les lignes sobres de la piscine de 17 mètres de long, construite avec des pierres provenant du village de montagne voisin, Ménerbes. Tout autour, du chèvrefeuille et des plantes vivaces résistantes à la sécheresse, comme le romarin et le thym, sont taillés en buissons.

Oben: die geraden Linien des 17 Meter langen Swimmingpools, der aus dem Stein des nahe gelegenen Bergdorfes Ménerbes erbaut wurde. Widerstandsfähige, gegen Trockenheit unempfindliche Kräuter wie Rosmarin und Thymian werden ebenso wie das immergrüne Geißblatt zu Formbäumchen geschnitten.

Above: the living room, where plants, flowers and even the stacks of firewood take on a particularly important decorative role. The chairs and the sculpture in the corner are both by the master of the house.
Right: a detail of a collection of Palestinian earthenware urns.

Ci-dessus: le salon, où les plantes, les fleurs et même les piles de bûches jouent un rôle décoratif particulièrement important. Les chaises et la sculpture dans l'angle sont l'œuvre du maître de maison.
A droite: un détail de la collection de poteries palestiniennes en terre cuite.

Oben: das Wohnzimmer, in dem Pflanzen, Blumen und sogar das aufgestapelte Feuerholz eine wichtige dekorative Funktion haben. Die Stühle und die Plastik in der Ecke stammen alle vom Hausherrn persönlich.
Rechts: ein Teil der Sammlung von Keramikamphoren aus Palästina.

Right: Beds and sofas alike are masked under heavy linen or cotton drapes.
Below: the dining-room with a table designed by the owner, and chairs in metal and straw, bought at L'Isle-sur-la-Sorgue. The two ornate columns were salvaged from the church at Mirabeau.

A droite: lits et sofas sont recouverts de lourds draps en lin ou en coton.
Ci-dessous: la salle à manger, avec une table dessinée par le maître de maison, et des chaises en métal et en paille achetées à l'Isle-sur-la-Sorgue. Les deux colonnes ouvragées ont été récupérées dans une église de Mirabeau.

Rechts: Betten und Sofas sind alle unter schweren Leinen- und Baumwollstoffen verborgen.
Unten: das Eßzimmer mit einem vom Hausherrn entworfenen Tisch sowie Stühlen aus Metall und Stroh, die in L'Isle-sur-la-Sorgue erworben wurden. Die beiden dekorativen Säulen wurden aus der Kirche von Mirabeau gerettet.

Above: *a view of the master bedroom, where the stone headboard doubles as a bedside table and is the main architectural statement in the room. The chair is Charles X and probably Provençal.*
Facing page: *the functional kitchen, where, as in the rest of the house, the walls are textured with limewash and sand. The curved work surface is in local marble.*

Ci-dessus: *une vue de la chambre de maître, où la tête de lit en pierre fait également office de table de chevet et constitue l'élément architectural principal de la pièce. La chaise, probablement provençale, est d'époque Charles X.*
Page de droite: *la cuisine, fonctionnelle, où, comme dans le reste de la maison, les murs sont enduits de chaux et de sable. Le plan de travail incurvé est en marbre de la région.*

Oben: *Ansicht des Schlafzimmers mit dem steinernen Kopfteil, das zugleich als Nachttisch dient und das wichtigste architektonische Element des Raumes darstellt. Der Stuhl ist aus der Zeit Karls X. und vermutlich provenzalisch.*
Rechte Seite: *Die funktionelle Küche, deren Wände ebenso wie im übrigen Haus mit Kalkanstrich und Sand aufgerauht sind. Die gebogene Arbeitsplatte besteht aus ortstypischem Marmor.*

This isolated priory on the winding road from Apt to Lourmarin has a fascinating history. Dating from the 11th century and long the religious centre of the area, it almost certainly had a military role as a watch tower – which explains its particularly tall steeple. It was classed as a historical monument by the writer Prosper Mérimée, when he was working for the French equivalent of the National Trust. Its history took a more rock n'roll turn when Roger Vadim gave it as a wedding present to his new wife – who was none other than Jane Fonda. From Fonda it passed to Vial who kept the Hollywood aspect of the story alive by entrusting the restoration to none other than his great friend the American society decorator Tony Ingrao. Ingrao and Vial did an extraordinary job of the rebuilding and decoration. The shell had been reduced to a ruin and it has taken twenty years of work to make the house comfortable. The basic scheme is now once again that of the 11th century: the 14th and 15th century alterations have been stripped away.

Daniel Vial

Ce prieuré isolé sur la route sinueuse qui mène d'Apt à Lourmarin a une histoire peu banale: construit au XIe siècle, il a longtemps été le centre religieux de la région. Il jouait certainement également un rôle militaire de tour de garde, ce qui explique son haut clocher. Classé par Prosper Mérimée à l'époque où celui-ci était inspecteur des monuments historiques, le bâtiment connut des heures plus «rock n'roll» quand Roger Vadim l'offrit en cadeau de noces à sa jeune épouse, qui n'était autre que Jane Fonda. L'actrice le céda ensuite à Daniel Vial qui entretint le côté hollywoodien de l'histoire en confiant la restauration à son grand ami, le décorateur du gratin américain: Tony Ingrao. Vial et Ingrao ont réalisé un extraordinaire travail de reconstruction et de décoration. Lorsqu'ils entamèrent les travaux, la bâtisse n'était plus qu'une ruine. Il leur a fallu vingt ans pour la rendre confortable. Les volumes intérieurs ont désormais retrouvé leur aspect du XIe siècle, les altérations des XIVe et XVe siècles ayant été effacées.

Die einsam gelegene Abtei an der kurvenreichen Straße zwischen Apt und Lourmarin hat eine faszinierende Geschichte. Gegründet wurde sie im 11. Jahrhundert und war lange geistliches Zentrum der Region. Sehr wahrscheinlich hatte sie überdies eine militärische Funktion als Wachturm, was ihren ungewöhnlich hohen Kirchturm erklären würde. Der Schriftsteller Prosper Mérimée stellte das Gebäude als Konservator französischen Kulturgutes unter Denkmalschutz. Später folgte sozusagen eine Rock'n Roll-Phase, als Roger Vadim die Abtei kaufte und seiner damaligen Braut zur Hochzeit schenkte – die niemand anders war als Jane Fonda. Sie verkaufte das Haus an Daniel Vial, der wiederum den Hollywood-Touch am Leben erhielt, indem er mit der Renovierung seinen Freund, den amerikanischen High-Society-Ausstatter Tony Ingrao, beauftragte. Ingrao und Vial gelangen Umbau und Gestaltung des Gebäudes ausgezeichnet. Die Außenmauern waren fast völlig verrottet, und es kostete zwanzig Jahre Arbeit, bis man wieder von einem komfortablen Wohnhaus sprechen konnte. Die Räume entsprechen heute wieder der Aufteilung des 11. Jahrhunderts, nachdem die Veränderungen aus dem 14. und 15. Jahrhundert entfernt worden sind.

On the previous pages: the view from the house over lavender fields.
Above: Vial's study adjacent to his bedroom and hidden partly
underground in the discreet extension cleverly built so that it cannot
be perceived from ground level. The bookcase originally belonged to
Montpellier University and the framed pictures are reproductions of
Leonardo da Vinci's drawings. The screen is an 18th-century "chinoiserie", such as the one in the bedroom on the top of the facing page.

Double page précédente: les champs de lavande vus de la maison.
Ci-dessus: le bureau de Vial, attenant à sa chambre. Il est partiellement enterré grâce à une extension discrète et astucieuse du bâtiment, invisible de l'extérieur. La bibliothèque appartenait autrefois à l'université de Montpellier et les dessins au mur sont des
reproductions d'esquisses de Léonard de Vinci. Le paravent est une
chinoiserie du XVIIIe siècle, tout comme celui de la chambre à la
page de droite.

Vorhergehende Doppelseite: Blick vom Haus aus über Lavendelfelder.
Oben: Vials Arbeitsraum neben seinem Schlafzimmer ist teilweise unter der Erde in einem diskreten Anbau untergebracht, der so geschickt
angelegt ist, daß man ihn vom Erdgeschoß aus nicht sieht. Der
Bücherschrank stand einst in der Universität von Montpellier, die gerahmten Bilder sind Reproduktionen von Zeichnungen Leonardo da
Vincis. Der Wandschirm ist eine Chinoiserie-Arbeit aus dem 18. Jahrhundert, ebenso wie das Pendant in dem auf der rechten Seite oben
abgebildeten Schlafzimmer.

Right: *the denim-trimmed four-poster in the guest bedroom.*
Below: *the kitchen, which features a sofa and armchairs draped in white linen in order not to detract from the splendid architecture of the priory.*

A droite: *le lit à baldaquin de la chambre d'amis, avec sa passementerie en jean.*
Ci-dessous: *la cuisine, avec un canapé et des fauteuils tapissés de lin blanc afin que l'œil ne soit pas distrait de la magnifique architecture du prieuré.*

Rechts: *das mit Jeansstoff besetzte Himmelbett im Gästezimmer.*
Unten: *die Küche. Sofa und Lehnstühle sind mit weißem Leinen bezogen, damit nichts von der herrlichen Architektur der Abtei ablenkt.*

This modern house designed by the architect Nasrine Faghih lies in 30 hectares of grounds in one of the most unspoilt parts of Provence. Between Apt and Forcalquier, on the way to Jean Giono's beloved highlands, on a site well protected from the mistral, the house is a haven of peace with a splendid view of the Lubéron. It has been conceived as a modernistic interpretation of a "bastide", a country house, incorporating certain Islamic precepts relative to the presence of water and the role of the home as a refuge from the outer world. The two swimming pools provide the illusion of an unbroken sheet of water linking the inside and out: The strong light that floods the minimalist interior is an integral element of the design, and the acoustics and disposal of the rooms all obey ancient rules that make for harmony. The illustration on the facing page shows a Martin Szekely table on the terrace.

Nasrine Faghih

Cette bâtisse moderne dessinée par l'architecte Nasrine Faghih se dresse sur un terrain de trente hectares situé entre Apt et Forcalquier, dans un des coins les mieux préservés de Provence. A l'abri du mistral, sur la route qui mène aux hautes terres chères à Jean Giono, c'est un havre de paix avec une vue splendide sur le Lubéron. Nasrine Faghih l'a conçue comme une bastide moderne, y intégrant certains principes islamiques liés à la présence de l'eau et au rôle de la maison comme refuge contre le monde extérieur. Les deux piscines donnent l'illusion d'un plan d'eau ininterrompu reliant l'intérieur et l'extérieur. La lumière qui inonde l'intérieur minimaliste est partie intégrante du décor et les pièces ont été créées selon des lois traditionnelles qui engendrent une atmosphère d'harmonie. L'illustration à la page de droite montre une table de Martin Szekely sur la terrasse.

Das von der Architektin Nasrine Faghih entworfene moderne Haus steht auf einem 30 Hektar großen Grundstück in einer der schönsten Gegenden der Provence. Zwischen Apt und Forcalquier, auf dem Weg zu dem von Jean Giono so verehrten Hochland, liegt das Gebäude in einer vor dem Mistral gut geschützten Stelle, wie ein Hort des Friedens mit prachtvoller Aussicht auf den Lubéron. Angelegt wurde das Haus als modernistische Form der »bastide«, wobei auch bestimmte islamische Prinzipien berücksichtigt wurden, etwa was die Bedeutung des Wassers und die Rolle des Heims als Ort des Rückzugs vor der Welt angeht. Die beiden Swimmingpools wecken die Illusion einer durchgehenden Wasserfläche, ohne Trennung zwischen innen und außen. Das harte Licht, das auf die minimalistische Einrichtung fällt, ist integraler Bestandteil des Designs. Akustik und Raumaufteilung folgen uralten Regeln der Harmonie. Die Abbildung auf der rechten Seite zeigt einen Tisch von Martin Szekely auf der Terrasse.

On the previous pages: a view of the inside swimming pool showing the sliding doors in metal and glass that connect the two pools.
Facing page: the bedroom with its narrow windows that look out onto a wooded slope, celebrated as being a great truffle-hunting ground.
Above: the living room that expresses the art of living simply surrounded by the minimum of possessions. The alcoves were designed specifically to house an impressive collection of paintings by Picasso.

Double page précédente: la piscine intérieure avec ses portes coulissantes à structure métallique qui s'ouvrent sur la piscine extérieure.
Page de gauche: la chambre à coucher avec ses fenêtres étroites qui donnent sur une colline boisée, connue pour être un excellent terrain truffier.
Ci-dessus: le salon, qui exprime l'art de vivre dans le dépouillement. Les alcôves ont été dessinées spécialement pour accueillir une impressionnante collection de tableaux de Picasso.

Vorhergehende Doppelseite: Blick über den Swimmingpool im Inneren des Hauses auf die Schiebetüren aus Metall und Glas, die beide Becken verbinden.
Linke Seite: Das Schlafzimmer mit den hohen, schmalen Fenstern blickt auf einen bewaldeten Hang, der als hervorragendes Trüffelgebiet gilt.
Oben: Das Wohnzimmer ist Ausdruck einer nur mit einem Minimum an Besitztümern auskommenden Lebenskunst. Die Nischen wurden eigens für die überragende Sammlung von Picasso-Gemälden konzipiert.

This troglodyte home, partly built in the living rock, is niched among the village Saignon's ancient foundations. Rosario Moreno and Aldo Franceschini arrived in 1964, via her native Argentina and Paris. A stone which happened to fall near the little square indicated that there might be a structure underneath a pile of ruins. In the excitement of the discovery, the land was bought for 500 francs, and the work on the house began. The young couple were penniless, to the point of not even being able to buy a proper spade. All the restoration and building work was done with improvised tools and a temperamental old Renault. They slowly managed to restore what turned out to be two giant vaulted cellars and eventually succeeded, with difficulty, in buying up the neighbouring ruins and restore them, acquiring enough space for a painter's studio, a terrace and a garden. It took them, with the help of Aldo's son, the best part of thirty years.

Rosario Moreno et Aldo Franceschini

Cette maison troglodyte, partiellement creusée dans le rocher, est nichée dans les anciennes fondations du village de Saignon. Rosario Moreno et Aldo Franceschini sont arrivés à Saignon en 1964, via l'Argentine et Paris. Une pierre, tombée accidentellement près de la petite place, leur a laissé deviner la présence d'une structure sous un tas de ruines. Excités par la perspective d'une découverte, ils achetèrent le terrain pour 500 francs et se mirent aussitôt à la tâche. Le jeune couple sans le sou n'avait pas même de quoi s'offrir une pelle digne de ce nom. Ils réalisèrent tous les travaux de restauration et de maçonnerie avec des outils de fortune et une vieille Renault caractérielle. Peu à peu, ils dégagèrent deux immenses caves voûtées. Ils parvinrent, non sans mal, a racheter les ruines adjacentes et à les restaurer, obtenant ainsi suffisamment d'espace pour créer un atelier de peintre, une terrasse et un jardin. Avec l'aide du fils d'Aldo, cela leur a demandé près de trente ans.

Dieses höhlenartige Haus, das zum Teil direkt in den Felsen hineingebaut wurde, liegt inmitten der alten Fundamente des Dorfes Saignon. Rosario Moreno und Aldo Franceschini kamen 1964 aus Argentinien und Paris hierher. Ein Stein, der an dem kleinen Dorfplatz zufällig herunterfiel, deutete darauf hin, daß sich unter einem Schutthaufen möglicherweise ein Gebäude verbarg. Begeistert von dem Fund kauften sie das Grundstück für 500 Francs und machten sich an die Arbeit. Das junge Paar besaß keinen Sou und konnte sich nicht einmal einen vernünftigen Spaten leisten. Die gesamten Instandsetzungs- und Bauarbeiten wurden mit improvisiertem Werkzeug und einem alten Renault vollbracht. Allmählich gelang es ihnen, zwei riesige Kellerräume mit Gewölben wiederherzustellen. Zu guter Letzt kauften sie unter großen Schwierigkeiten auch die angrenzenden Ruinen auf und restaurierten sie ebenfalls, so daß nun Platz für ein Atelier, eine Terrasse und einen Garten vorhanden ist. Alles in allem kostete sie das ganze Projekt fast dreißig Jahre.

On these pages: Rosario Moreno's studio. These magestically proportioned stone cellars are probably the oldest structures in the village. Although Rosario Moreno bought the land and the ruins from a total of eight different owners in eight separate deals over fifteen or so years, it is believed that they could have all been part of the same property originally. Rosario Moreno was something of a trail blazer for the many artists who were to flock to the Lubéron in the seventies, many of whom encountered the same resistance as she did when she first decided to settle there.
On the following pages: the kitchen.

Page de gauche, ci-dessus et ci-dessous: l'atelier de Rosario Moreno. Ces caves en pierres aux proportions majestueuses sont sans doute les plus anciennes structures du village. Bien que Rosario Moreno ait racheté les terres et les ruines de huit propriétaires différents sur une période d'une quinzaine d'années, ces dernières pourraient autrefois avoir fait partie d'une même propriété. Rosario fait figure de pionnière pour les nombreux artistes qui ont envahi le Lubéron dans les années soixante-dix. La plupart se sont heurtés aux mêmes obstacles qu'elle lorsqu'elle a décidé de s'installer dans le village.
Double page suivante: la cuisine.

Diese Doppelseite: Rosario Morenos Atelier. Die majestätisch proportionierten Kellergewölbe dürften die ältesten Bauteile des Dorfes sein. Auch wenn Rosario Moreno Grundstück und Ruinen von insgesamt acht Eigentümern zusammenkaufte, wofür acht einzelne Kaufverträge und rund fünfzehn Jahre erforderlich waren, geht man davon aus, daß alles ursprünglich zu einem einzigen Besitz gehörte. Rosario Moreno bereitete in gewisser Weise den Weg für viele Künstler, die es in den siebziger Jahren in den Lubéron zog, wenn auch viele von ihnen mit den gleichen Widerständen zu kämpfen hatten wie sie selbst, als sie beschloß, sich hier niederzulassen.
Folgende Doppelseite: die Küche.

The Rocchias come close to living the rural idyll that foreigners imagine when they dream of Provence. Sheltered by Cézanne's beloved mountain, the Mont Sainte-Victoire (see pp. 208/209) their little cabin overflows with the produce of the countryside. Jean-Marie is Provence's truffle expert, author of a popular book on the subject of the "black diamond", as he refers to it. He is also the proud owner of a very large, very greedy and inordinately friendly truffle pig, which has rather taken over the garden. She – for the 200-kilo gourmet is a she – has to share a pen with a gaggle of geese who were originally introduced with the aim of producing "foie gras"; these became awfully friendly with the family and thus were spared a fate worse than death. If Jean-Marie has been truffle hunting since the age of seven, his wife has been keeping bees for 16 years. She decants the delicately scented honey from her 120 hives which are placed in what has to be one of the least frequented but most breathtaking beauty spots in the region, with a perfect view of the Mont Sainte-Victoire.

Jean-Marie et Jennifer Rocchia

La vie des Rocchia ressemble un peu à ce rêve bucolique que font les étrangers quand ils pensent à la Provence. A l'abri de la montagne Sainte-Victoire chère à Cézanne (voir pp. 208/209), leur petit cabanon regorge des produits de la nature. Jean-Marie est l'expert en truffes de la Provence, auteur d'un livre sur «le diamant noir», comme il l'appelle. Il est également l'heureux propriétaire d'une énorme truie, très gloutonne et fort sympathique, qui règne en maîtresse sur le jardin. Cette gourmande de 200 kg partage toutefois ses quartiers avec un troupeau d'oies. A l'origine, ces dernières étaient destinées à finir en foie gras, mais elles ont témoigné tant d'affection à la famille qu'on leur a épargné cette mort cruelle. Si Jean-Marie chasse la truffe depuis l'âge de sept ans, sa femme élève des abeilles depuis 16 ans. Elle draine un miel au parfum délicat de ses 120 ruches dans un des plus beaux décors naturels de Provence, avec sa vue idéale sur la fameuse montagne.

Das Leben der Rocchias kommt der bäuerlichen Idylle, von der Ausländer beim Gedanken an die Provence träumen, sehr nahe. Im Schutze der von Cézanne geliebten Montagne Sainte-Victoire (s. S. 208/209) quillt ihr Häuschen fast über von den landwirtschaftlichen Produkten der Region. Jean-Marie ist der Trüffelexperte der Provence und Autor eines populären Buches über den »schwarzen Diamanten«, wie er die Trüffel nennt. Außerdem ist er stolzer Besitzer eines sehr großen, sehr freßgierigen und ausgesprochen freundlichen Trüffelschweins, das den Garten mehr oder weniger in Beschlag genommen hat. Sie – es handelt sich nämlich genaugenommen um eine Trüffelsau – muß ihren Koben mit einer Schar Gänse teilen, die ursprünglich für die Produktion von Gänsestopfleber angeschafft wurden, bis sich zwischen ihnen und der Familie eine wahre Freundschaft entwickelte und man ihnen ihr schreckliches Schicksal ersparte. Während Jean-Marie seit seinem siebten Lebensjahr Trüffel sammelt, ist seine Frau seit 16 Jahren Imkerin. Sie bereitet den zart duftenden Honig ihrer 120 Bienenvölker auf, die in einer der am wenigsten bekannten, dafür aber landschaftlich schönsten Ecken der Region mit wundervoller Aussicht auf die Montagne Sainte-Victoire stehen.

On the previous pages: *view of the Mont Sainte-Victoire.*
Facing page and above: *two of the bedrooms with their tiled floors,
wooden beams and white cotton drapes. The "cabanon", which was
originally a rudimentary weekend cottage of the kind favoured by the
working classes in the larger Provençal towns and primarily used for
staging long Sunday picnic lunches, was restored and enlarged by the
Rocchias 25 years ago. It is simply furnished with a few chosen pieces
of Provençal furniture.*
Following pages: *the kitchen cupboard and its array of local
ceramics, and a niche in the outhouse.*

Double page précédente: *vue sur la montagne Sainte-Victoire.*
Page de gauche et ci-dessus: *deux des chambres, avec leur sol carrelé, leurs poutres apparentes et leurs rideaux en coton blanc. Le cabanon, au départ une petite maison de week-end comme les aiment
les ouvriers des grandes villes de Provence pour y faire de longs pique-
niques dominicaux, a été restauré et agrandi par les Rocchia il y a
25 ans. Il est meublé simplement avec quelques meubles provençaux
bien choisis.*
Pages suivantes: *les étagères de la cuisine avec une collection de
céramiques de la région et une niche dans la resserre.*

Vorhergehende Doppelseite: *Blick auf die Montagne Sainte-
Victoire.*
Linke Seite und oben: *zwei der Schlafzimmer mit ihren gefliesten
Fußböden, Holzbalken und weißen Baumwollgardinen. Der »caba-
non«, ursprünglich ein ganz schlichtes Wochenendhäuschen von der
Art, wie sie die Arbeiter der großen provenzalischen Städte vor allem
für ausgedehnte sonntägliche Picknicks nutzten, wurde von den
Rocchias vor 25 Jahren renoviert und vergrößert. Es ist mit
wenigen provenzalischen Möbelstücken zweckmäßig eingerichtet.*
Folgende Seiten: *der Küchenschrank mit seiner Auswahl ortsüblicher
Keramik; eine Nische im Nebengebäude.*

A few years ago, conscious that the Pascal family property at the foot of the Lubéron mountains not far from Aix was slowly but surely falling into ruin, Franck and Marc took the decision to abandon their Parisian existence for good and took up residence at Arnajon. The house was originally a Louis XIV hunting lodge, converted into a "bastide" during the 18th century and finally fitted out and furnished as a rural pleasure palace, complete with a shell grotto, winter garden and majestic fountains in the 19th century. It is the remains of this latter incarnation that convey a slightly Italianate atmosphere to the estate. While wandering along the balustraded terraces you feel as if on the other side of the Alps, by a Venetian lagoon or in the rolling Tuscan hills. Franck and Marc now spend half their time in Italy, and so are well placed to exploit the spirit of that country.

Franck Pascal et Marc Heracle

Il y a quelques années, conscients que la maison de famille des Pascal au pied des montagnes du Lubéron était lentement mais sûrement en train de tomber en ruines, Franck et Marc prirent la grave décision d'abandonner définitivement leur vie parisienne pour s'installer à Arnajon. Située non loin d'Aix, la maison est un ancien relais de chasse Louis XIV, transformé en bastide au XVIIIe siècle puis embelli et reconverti au XIXe siècle en demeure campagnade, avec grotte en coquillages, jardin d'hiver et fontaines majestueuses. Ce sont les restes de cette dernière incarnation qui donnent à la propriété son air légèrement italianisant. En se promenant sur les terrasses à balustrade, on peut s'imaginer de l'autre côté des Alpes, au bord d'un lagon vénitien ou sur les collines de Toscane. Franck et Marc passent désormais la moitié de leur temps en Italie, c'est donc en connaisseurs qu'ils se sont inspirés de l'esprit de ce pays pour créer les décors d'Arnajon.

Als Franck und Marc vor einigen Jahren klar wurde, daß der Familienbesitz der Pascals unweit von Aix am Fuße des Lubérons langsam, aber unerbittlich dem Verfall entgegenging, beschlossen die beiden, ihr Pariser Leben für immer aufzugeben und sich in Arnajon niederzulassen. Das Haus war ursprünglich ein Jagdschloß Ludwigs XIV., wurde im 18. Jahrhundert in eine »bastide« umgewandelt und schließlich als ländliches Lustschlößchen hergerichtet, zu dem man im 19. Jahrhundert noch eine Muschelgrotte, einen Wintergarten und gewaltige Brunnen hinzufügte. Die Reste dieser späteren Verwandlung vermitteln noch heute eine leicht italienische Atmosphäre. Wenn man die balustradenbewehrten Terrassen entlangwandert, fühlt man sich fast wie jenseits der Alpen, an einer venezianischen Lagune oder inmitten sanfter toskanischer Hügel. Franck und Marc verbringen inzwischen die Hälfte ihrer Zeit in Italien und besitzen insofern hervorragende Voraussetzungen, den Geist dieses Landes in die Gestaltung ihres Schlosses einfließen zu lassen.

On the previous pages: *a view of a 19th-century summer house in the grounds, not yet restored. The detail shows one of Franck and Marc's friendly little donkeys whose function is that of an amiable lawn mower.*
Above and detail right: *a festive table for a summer buffet in the garden.*

Pages précédentes: *un pavillon d'été du XIXe siècle sur la propriété, en attente d'être restauré. Le détail montre un des gentils ânes de Franck et Marc, qui font également office de tondeuse à gazon.*
Ci-dessus et détail de droite: *une table de fête pour un buffet estival dans le jardin.*

Vorhergehende Seiten: *das im 19. Jahrhundert auf dem Anwesen errichtete Sommerhaus, das noch nicht renoviert wurde. Das Detail zeigt eines von Francks und Marcs freundlichen Eselchen, die als liebenswerte Rasenmäher fungieren.*
Oben und Detail rechts: *der für ein sommerliches Buffet im Garten festlich gedeckte Tisch.*

Below and on the following pages: a view of the orangery, adjacent to the house and now restored to what is probably rather more than its former splendour, thanks to the owners' talents for "trompe l'œil". This contemporary fantasy of what a winter garden should be succeeds in evoking the 19th-century atmosphere of when it was built.

Ci-dessous et double page suivante: l'orangerie attenante à la maison a désormais retrouvé sa splendeur d'autrefois, sinon plus, grâce au talent des propriétaires pour le trompe-l'œil. Cette vision contemporaine de ce que devait être un jardin d'hiver évoque parfaitement l'atmosphère du XIXe siècle, époque où l'orangerie fut construite.

Unten und folgende Doppelseite: die an das Haus angrenzende Orangerie, die inzwischen dank Francks und Marcs meisterhafter Beherrschung der Trompe-l'œil-Technik schöner hergerichtet ist, als sie vermutlich je war. Auch wenn es eine heutige Phantasie war, die hier einen idealen Wintergarten schuf, so wird doch die Atmosphäre des 19. Jahrhundert spürbar, die Zeit, in der die Orangerie errichtet wurde.

Facing page and above: *two views of the large country kitchen where the vast collection of Provençal and Italian ceramics has been made the principal element of the decor. The accumulation of plates, jugs, statuettes and kitchen utensils conspire to give a highly theatrical atmosphere to this otherwise simply furnished and functional room, which is the true heart of the house.*

Page de gauche et ci-dessus: *la grande cuisine campagnarde, véritable cœur de la maison, où la vaste collection de céramiques provençales et italiennes constitue l'élément principal du décor. L'accumulation d'assiettes, de jarres, de statuettes et d'ustensiles de cuisine crée une atmosphère très théâtrale dans cette pièce pourtant fonctionnelle et meublée simplement.*

Linke Seite und oben: *zwei Ansichten der großen bäuerlichen Küche mit einer riesigen Sammlung provenzalischer und italienischer Keramik, die zum wesentlichen dekorativen Element geworden ist. Das Nebeneinander von Tellern, Krügen, Statuetten und Küchengeräten erzeugt eine hochdramatische Atmosphäre in dem ansonsten schlicht eingerichteten, funktionalen Raum, der das eigentliche Kernstück des Hauses bildet.*

Abandoning Paris for the provincial charms of Aix-en-Provence and life in this perfectly proportioned 18th-century "bastide" was a bold but inspired decision for Armand Hadida and his family. He still spends a considerable amount of time in the capital where his intelligently conceived shops, known as "L'Eclaireur", are favourite addresses of fashionable Parisians. Alongside the designer clothes he features chosen furniture and objects by Fornasetti, Frank O. Gehry and the design duo Mathieu and Ray, among others. Paul Mathieu and Michael Ray are also based in Aix, and it was to them that Hadida turned for the decoration of his Provençal home. The house combines the advantages of being very close to the centre of town with the charm of the countryside. Hadida had a clear idea of what he wanted and took a personal interest in the decoration. With Mathieu and Ray he has succeeded in bringing the old house back to life.

Martine et Armand Hadida

Pour Armand Hadida et sa famille, quitter Paris pour les charmes provinciaux d'Aix-en-Provence et s'installer dans cette bastide du XVIIIe siècle fut une décision audacieuse mais inspirée. Hadida continue de consacrer un temps considérable à ses boutiques parisiennes, «L'Eclaireur». Conçues avec intelligence, elles sont une des adresses préférées du Tout-Paris. Aux côtés de vêtements de créateurs, il y présente des meubles et des objets de designers dont Fornasetti, Frank O. Gehry et le duo Mathieu et Ray. Paul Mathieu et Michael Ray habitant aussi à Aix, c'est naturellement vers eux qu'Hadida s'est tourné pour la décoration de sa maison provençale. Cette bâtisse aux proportions parfaites associe l'avantage d'être à deux pas du centre ville avec les charmes de la campagne. Lorsqu'il l'a découverte en 1990, Hadida avait une idée très précise de ce qu'il souhaitait. Il s'est intéressé de près à la décoration et, avec Mathieu et Ray, il est parvenu à ramener la vieille maison à la vie.

Paris den Rücken zu kehren, es gegen die provinziellen Reize von Aix-en-Provence einzutauschen und in einer perfekt proportionierten »bastide« aus dem 18. Jahrhundert zu leben – dies war für Armand Hadida und seine Familie ein kühner, aber wohlüberlegter Schritt. Noch immer verbringt er einen Gutteil seiner Zeit in der Hauptstadt, wo seine intelligent aufgemachten Läden unter dem Namen »L'Eclaireur« zu den beliebtesten Adressen für modebewußte Pariser gehören. Neben Designerkleidung führt er exquisite Möbel und Objekte, unter anderem von Fornasetti, Frank O. Gehry und dem Designerduo Mathieu und Ray. Da Paul Mathieu und Michael Ray ebenfalls in Aix leben, wandte sich Hadida wegen der Ausstattung seines provenzalischen Hauses an sie. Er hatte sehr genaue Vorstellungen von dem, was er wollte, und beschäftigte sich persönlich mit der Innenausstattung. Gemeinsam mit Mathieu und Ray gelang es ihm, dem alten Haus neues Leben einzuhauchen.

Above: the dining-room where Mathieu's imagination and sense of poetry shine forth from the details on the specially commissioned furniture. The table is in walnut, and the carved frieze was an idea of Hadida's. The lamp was designed for the room and custom-made in Marseille, where the glass was blown.
Below: The dresser displays Fornasetti's "Adam and Eve" plates.
Facing page: details of the specially made pieces.
On the following pages: a view of the living room, with the rather grand 19th-century columns which came with the house. The furniture and the carpets are by Mathieu and Ray.

Ci-dessus: la salle à manger, où l'imagination de Mathieu et son sens poétique transparaissent dans les moindres détails des meubles créés tout spécialement. La table est en noyer. La frise sculptée est une idée d'Hadida. Le lustre en verre soufflé a été dessiné pour la pièce et réalisé sur mesure à Marseille.
Ci-dessous: Le vaisselier présente la série d'assiettes de Fornasetti, «Adam et Eve».
Page de droite: des détails des meubles conçus spécialement.
Double page suivante: le salon, avec les élégantes colonnes du XIXe siècle qui se trouvaient déjà dans la maison. Les meubles et les tapis sont de Mathieu et de Ray.

Oben: das Eßzimmer, in dem Mathieus Phantasie und Sinn für Poesie noch in den Details des Mobiliars zutage treten. Der Tisch ist aus Walnußholz, dessen geschnitzter Fries eine Idee Hadidas. Die extra für diesen Raum entworfene Lampe wurde in Marseille nach Maß angefertigt, dort wurden auch die Glasteile mundgeblasen.
Unten: In dem Regal stehen Fornasettis Teller »Adam und Eva«.
Rechte Seite: Details der eigens angefertigten Möbelstücke.
Folgende Doppelseite: Blick ins Wohnzimmer mit den wuchtigen Säulen aus dem 19. Jahrhundert, die bereits zur früheren Ausstattung gehörten. Möbel und Teppiche stammen von Mathieu und Ray.

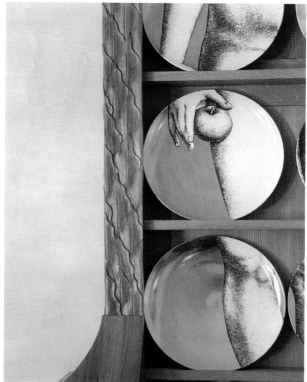

Above: *a detail of the inlaid sideboard, with its "organic" carvings. The figures are partly allegorical creations of Mathieu and Ray.*
Facing page, clockwise from top left: *an 18th-century carving above the piano in the living room; a dolphin motif on the carpet; damask curtains by Rubelli; the leaf motif, often repeated throughout the house.*

Ci-dessus: *un détail du buffet marqueté, dont les motifs représentent des formes anthropomorphes dessinées par Mathieu et Ray.*
Page de droite, en haut à gauche: *un bois sculpté du XVIIIe siècle au-dessus du piano du salon; puis dans le sens des aiguilles d'une montre: un motif du tapis représentant un dauphin; des rideaux damassés de chez Rubelli; un motif de feuille, que l'on retrouve partout dans la maison.*

Oben: *Ausschnitt aus der mit Einlegearbeiten versehenen Anrichte, die »organische« Schnitzereien aufweist. Die Figuren sind zum Teil allegorische Kreationen von Mathieu und Ray.*
Rechte Seite, im Uhrzeigersinn von oben links: *eine Schnitzarbeit aus dem 18. Jahrhundert über dem Flügel im Wohnzimmer; das Delphinmotiv des Teppichs; Damastvorhänge von Rubelli; das Blattmotiv, das sich im ganzen Haus mehrfach wiederholt.*

Facing page: *one of the pair of inlaid maple-wood desks in the bedroom of the Hadidas' two youngest daughters.*
Above: *an overall view of their bedroom, with a forties' mirrored chest of drawers and an original lighting fixture bought at L'Isle-sur-la-Sorgue. The smaller ones on either side of the beds were specially made to reproduce the design.*

Page de gauche: *un des deux bureaux en érable marqueté de la chambre des deux benjamines Hadida.*
Ci-dessus: *une vue générale de la chambre, avec une commode à trumeau des années quarante et des appliques originales chinées à L'Isle-sur-la-Sorgue. Des copies plus petites de ces dernières ont été placées de part et d'autre des lits.*

Linke Seite: *einer der beiden Ahornschreibtische mit Einlegearbeiten im Schlafzimmer der beiden jüngsten Hadida-Töchter.*
Oben: *Gesamtansicht ihres Schlafzimmers mit einer Spiegelkommode aus den vierziger Jahren und einer originellen Lampe, die in L'Isle-sur-la-Sorgue gekauft wurde. Die kleineren Lampen auf beiden Seiten der Betten wurden eigens als passende Pendants angefertigt.*

Above: the kitchen which looks as if it has been there for ever but in fact was entirely re-designed: doors were moved, the floor was laid, and the ceiling was raised.
Facing page, clockwise from top left: details of the wooden kitchen fittings carved with the text of a poem by Mistral; little glass vases by Bořek Šípek; the chicken wire on the doors; the lid of the elegant waste-disposal chute; a carved olive branch.

Ci-dessus: la cuisine, entièrement redécorée même si elle semble avoir toujours été ainsi: les portes ont été déplacées, le sol a été refait et le plafond rehaussé.
Page de droite, en haut à gauche: un détail des tiroirs du buffet sur lesquels est gravé un poème de Frédéric Mistral; puis dans le sens des aiguilles d'une montre: des petits vases en verre de Bořek Šípek; le grillage à poule des portes du buffet; le couvercle de l'élégant vide-ordures; une branche d'olivier sculptée.

Oben: Die Küche wirkt so, als habe sie nie anders ausgesehen, wurde jedoch in Wirklichkeit völlig neu konzipiert. Dafür wurden Türen versetzt, die Bodenfliesen gelegt und die Decke erhöht.
Rechte Seite, im Uhrzeigersinn von oben links: Details der hölzernen Kücheneinrichtung, in die der Text eines Gedichtes von Mistral geschnitzt ist; kleine Glasvasen von Bořek Šípek; die mit Maschendraht versehenen Schranktüren; der Deckel des eleganten Müllschluckers; ein geschnitzter Olivenzweig.

While house-hunting in Provence, Lillian Williams and her husband spotted this 17th-century pavilion. They were looking to buy a "hotel particulier" in Aix in order to display Lillian's extensive costume collection. Costumes, notably those of the 18th century, are Lillian's passion and she has lent pieces for her collection to several museums including the Metropolitan. Smitten by the gracious proportions, the charming steps framing the garden façade, and the classically appointed "jardin à l'italienne", complete with fountains and terraces, they acquired the property and Lillian set about transforming it into the perfect, 18th-century "folie". Her taste for the theatrical is here translated in a Baroque interior, where dressed mannequins are displayed in order to evoke Provençal life two hundred years ago. It is this fascination with the daily occurrences, the small details of the "quotidien" (on which she is writing a book), that distinguishes Lillian's collection and gives it a particular vitality.

Lillian Williams

Lillian Williams et son mari ont découvert ce pavillon du XVIIe siècle tandis qu'ils cherchaient un hôtel particulier à Aix pour accueillir la vaste collection de costumes de Lillian. Les costumes, notamment ceux du XVIIIe siècle, sont la passion de Lillian qui a prêté certaines de ses pièces à plusieurs musées, dont le Metropolitan de New York. Séduits par les proportions gracieuses du bâtiment, la charmante «descente d'escalier» de la façade côté jardin et le jardin classique à l'italienne, avec son assortiment de terrasses et de fontaines, les Williams ont acheté la propriété, que Lillian s'est aussitôt mise à transformer en parfaite «folie» du XVIIIe siècle. Son goût pour le théâtral s'est traduit ici par un décor baroque, dans lequel des mannequins habillés font revivre la Provence d'il y a deux cents ans. C'est cette fascination pour la vie de l'époque, les petits détails du quotidien (sur lesquels elle est en train d'écrire un livre), qui font de la collection de Lillian quelque chose d'aussi vivant.

Auf der Suche nach einem Haus in der Provence entdeckten Lillian Williams und ihr Mann dieses Schlößchen aus dem 17. Jahrhundert. Eigentlich hatten sie vorgehabt, eine Stadtvilla in Aix zu kaufen, um Lillians umfangreiche Kostümsammlung unterbringen zu können. Historische Kostüme, vor allem aus dem 18. Jahrhundert, sind Lillians Leidenschaft, und Stücke aus ihrer Sammlung gingen schon als Leihgabe an verschiedene Museen. Begeistert von den anmutigen Proportionen, der hübschen Treppenanlage auf der Gartenseite und der klassischen italienischen Gartenanlage mit Brunnen und Terrassen kauften sie den Besitz, und Lillian übernahm es, ihn wieder in eine perfekte »folie« des 18. Jahrhunderts zu verwandeln. Ihr Sinn für Dramatik findet hier Ausdruck in der barocken Innenausstattung und den kostümierten Schaufensterpuppen, die das provenzalische Leben vor zweihundert Jahren verkörpern. Gerade die Faszination, die von den alltäglichen Dingen, den Kleinigkeiten des täglichen Lebens ausgeht – sie schreibt an einem Buch über das Phänomen des »quotidien«, des Alltäglichen –, zeichnet Lillians Sammlung aus und verleiht ihr eine besondere Vitalität.

Above: *a view of the classically appointed ornamental pond with a lavender field in the background – a reference to the Provençal countryside that was planted before the Williams bought the house.*
Facing page: *a view of what was originally a private theatre in the garden with a "tromp l'œil" in "azulejos".*
On the following pages: *a view of the "Salon des Chinoiseries", dominated by 18th-century terracotta statuettes of nodding mandarins and a late 17th-century Venetian harpsichord. The acid-yellow curtain silk was picked up from a dress manufacturer in Paris, as the right shade was simply not avaliable in furnishing fabric.*

Ci-dessus: *l'alignement classique du bassin et, derrière, un champ de lavande typiquement provençal qui était déjà là quand les Williams ont acheté la maison.*
Page de droite: *l'ancien petit théâtre privé dans le jardin, avec un trompe l'œil en azulejos.*
Double page suivante: *le «salon des chinoiseries», dominé par des statuettes de mandarins articulées en terre cuite datant du XVIIIe siècle et une harpe vénitienne de la fin du XVIIe siècle. Les rideaux en soie jaune acidulé ont été choisis chez un fabricant parisien d'étoffes de confection, la teinte désirée étant introuvable parmi les tissus d'ameublement.*

Oben: *Blick auf den klassisch angelegten Teich, im Hintergrund ein Lavendelfeld, ein beim Kauf bereits vorhandener Anklang an die provenzalische Landschaft.*
Rechte Seite: *Blick auf das ehemalige private Theater im Garten, das mit »Azulejo«-Kacheln in Trompe-l'œil-Technik ausgestattet ist.*
Folgende Doppelseite: *Blick in den »Salon des chinoiseries«, der von nickenden Mandarinen (Terrakottastatuen aus dem 18. Jahrhundert) und einem venezianischen Cembalo (aus dem späten 17. Jahrhundert) beherrscht wird. Die giftgelbe Vorhangseide wurde bei einer Kleiderfabrik in Paris gekauft, da es den richtigen Farbton als Dekostoff einfach nicht gab.*

Above: in the vaulted former stables, an arrangement of Neapolitan 18th-century nativity figures, and an architectural piece of the same period, probably also used in nativities. In the background, lifesized secular figures, that originally belonged to the Dukes of Bologna in the 16th century.
Facing page, clockwise from top left: a Louis XVI bed "à la Polonaise" frames a Provençal portrait of a girl; neatly tied bundles of "Le Mercure de France", the daily newspaper from the reign of Louis XIV; a King Charles spaniel on its very grand doggy bed; a detail of one of the mandarins in the Chinese salon.
On the following pages: a tent-like room, in striped fabric, entirely "Directoire", with further pieces from the impressive collection of antique musical instruments.

Ci-dessus: dans les anciennes écuries voûtées, une collection de santons napolitains du XVIIIe siècle et une maquette de la même époque, sans doute utilisée elle aussi dans les crèches. En arrière-plan, des statues grandeur nature qui appartenaient aux ducs de Bologne au XVIe siècle.
Page de droite, en haut à gauche: un lit Louis XVI à la polonaise dont le baldaquin encadre un portrait provençal de jeune fille; puis dans le sens des aiguilles d'une montre: des piles joliment nouées du «Mercure de France», un quotidien datant de Louis XIV; un king-charles sur une couche royale digne de lui; un des mandarins du salon chinois.
Double page suivante: un salon façon tente en tissu rayé, entièrement Directoire, et d'autres pièces de l'impressionnante collection d'instruments de musique anciens.

Oben: In den mit Gewölben versehenen ehemaligen Ställen sieht man ein Stilleben mit neapolitanischen Krippenfiguren aus dem 18. Jahrhundert und ein Architekturmodell aus der gleichen Epoche, das wahrscheinlich ebenfalls im Rahmen einer Krippe verwendet wurde. Im Hintergrund lebensgroße profane Figuren aus dem 16. Jahrhundert, die ursprünglich den Herzögen von Bologna gehörten.
Rechte Seite, im Uhrzeigersinn von links oben: Ein Louis-Seize-Baldachinbett umrahmt das Porträt eines provenzalischen Mädchens; sauber gebündelte Ausgaben des »Mercure de France«, einer Tageszeitung aus der Zeit Ludwigs XIV.; einer von mehreren King-Charles-Spaniels in seinem überaus prunkvollen Himmelbett; einer der Mandarine aus dem chinesischen Salon.
Folgende Doppelseite: ein zeltartiger, mit gestreiftem Stoff vollständig im Directoire-Stil eingerichteter Salon mit weiteren Stücken der eindrucksvollen Sammlung alter Musikinstrumente.

Facing page: A Baroque marble sink dominates a luxuriously appointed "cabinet de toilette" in pistachio and pale rose that features a gold vermeil bath, made for the famous Parisian courtesan who was mistress of the Prince of Wales in the late 19th century.
Above: Lillian William's pink bedroom. The fabric was specially commissioned from Manuel Canovas and based on an 18th-century design from her extensive collection.

Page de gauche: Un lavabo baroque en marbre domine le luxueux cabinet de toilette pistache et rose pâle. La baignoire en vermeil fut fabriquée pour une célèbre courtisane parisienne, maîtresse du Prince de Galles à la fin du XIXe siècle.
Ci-dessus: la chambre rose de Lillian Williams. Le tissu, commandé spécialement chez Manuel Canovas, reproduit un motif dix-huitième de la collection de costumes de la maîtresse de maison.

Linke Seite: Ein barockes Marmorwaschbecken beherrscht das luxuriös, pistaziengrün und blaßrosa ausgestattete »Cabinet de toilette«, zu dem auch eine vergoldete Email-Badewanne gehört. Sie wurde für die berühmte Pariser Kurtisane angefertigt, die im späten 19. Jahrhundert Mätresse des Prinzen von Wales war.
Oben: Lillians rosa Schlafzimmer. Der Stoff wurde eigens bei Manuel Canovas gefertigt und greift ein Muster des 18. Jahrhunderts aus ihrer umfangreichen Sammlung auf.

The gracious property Domaine de Souviou is situated at the foot of the mountainous Sainte-Baume, between Aix-en-Provence and Toulon. When the Cagnolaris first visited, it was a pile of ruins. Despite their busy Parisian life, and with the help of the architect Xavier Tronel and the decorator Patrice Nourissat, the house has now been restored to its former glory. The walls and ceilings were given rounded contours, the inside was painted olive, ochre and cream, wooden floors and floor-tiles were laid and a large dining-room-cum-kitchen installed, along with several bathrooms. The grounds have become fruitful once again and produce not only three different fine olive oils but also red, white and rosé Bandol wine under the label of the property. After almost ten years of work on the estate, the Cagnolaris have even fulfilled their pet ambition: to produce a "grand cru", a noble wine aged in their own cellars.

Christiane et Serge Cagnolari

La première fois que les Cagnolari ont visité l'élégant Domaine de Souviou, situé au pied du massif de la Sainte-Baume, entre Aix-en-Provence et Toulon, il n'était plus qu'un tas de ruines. En dépit de leur vie parisienne fort chargée, et avec l'aide de l'architecte Xavier Tronel et du décorateur Patrice Nourissat, ils lui ont redonné sa splendeur d'autrefois. Les contours des murs et des plafonds ont été arrondis, l'intérieur a été peint en vert olive, ocre et blanc cassé, les sols ont été recouverts de parquets ou de tomettes, une grande cuisine-salle à manger a été créée, ainsi que plusieurs salles de bains. La terre a retrouvé sa fertilité d'antan et produit, outre trois sortes d'excellentes huiles d'olive, du Bandol rosé, blanc et rouge qui porte le nom du domaine. Après dix années de travail sur la propriété, les Cagnolari ont enfin réalisé un de leurs rêves: produire un grand cru qui vieillisse dans leur propres caves.

Das schöne Anwesen Domaine de Souviou liegt am Fuß des Sainte-Baume-Massivs zwischen Aix-en-Provence und Toulon. Als die Cagnolaris das Haus zum erstenmal besichtigten, war es eine einzige Ruine, doch ihrem anstrengendem Pariser Leben zum Trotz sorgten sie mit Hilfe des Architekten Xavier Tronel und des Innenausstatters Patrice Nourissat dafür, daß es in seiner früheren Pracht wieder auferstehen durfte. Wände und Decken wurden abgerundet, das Innere olivgrün, ocker und cremefarben gestrichen, Holzdielen und »tommette«-Fliesen gelegt und eine große Wohnküche sowie mehrere Badezimmer geschaffen. Auch der Erdboden ringsherum wurde wieder fruchtbar gemacht und liefert nicht nur drei verschiedene edle Olivenöle, sondern darüber hinaus Bandol-Wein in Rot, Weiß und Rosé, der unter dem Namen des Gutes verkauft wird. Nach fast zehnjähriger Arbeit auf dem Anwesen ist es den Cagnolaris sogar gelungen, ihr ehrgeizigstes Vorhaben zu verwirklichen: einen Grand Cru zu produzieren, einen wahrhaft noblen, in ihrem eigenen Keller gereiften Wein.

Previous pages and above: views of the garden, which is delicately pretty and generously planted with a wealth of Mediterranean flowering plants and trees.
Facing page: the table set for lunch under the "tonelle".
Right: a detail of the "Domaine de Souviou" wines and the oils produced by the century-old olive trees in the grounds.

Pages précédentes et ci-dessus: différentes vues du jardin, d'une beauté délicate et accueillant une abondance de plantes à fleurs et d'arbres méditerranéens.
Page de gauche: le déjeuner servi sous la tonnelle.
A droite: les vins du «Domaine de Souviou» et les huiles produites par les oliviers centenaires.

Vorhergehende Seiten und oben: Ansichten des Gartens, der ausnehmend hübsch hergerichtet und üppig mit mediterranen Gewächsen und Bäumen bepflanzt ist.
Linke Seite: Unter der Laube ist der Tisch für das Mittagessen gedeckt.
Rechts: Einige der Weine der »Domaine de Souviou« und ihrer Öle, die aus den Früchten der eigenen jahrhundertealten Olivenbäume gepreßt werden.

Above and facing page: two views of the ochre and olive master bedroom. The frieze on the wall evokes Piero della Francesca, and indeed the atmosphere recalls that of an Italian "palazzo".
Detail bottom right: the bathroom designed by Xavier Tronel, with its tiled terracotta floor. The stone in which the sinks and the bath have been fitted has been treated with linseed oil. The three pineframed mirrors add to the graphic impact of the room.
On the following pages: the welcoming kitchen, one of the key rooms in the house. Designed by Patrice Nourissat and built in tinted pine by a local craftsman, the main piece of furniture is a large farmhouse table around which family and friends congregate for informal meals.

Ci-dessus et page de droite: la chambre de maître vert olive et ocre. La frise à la Piero della Francesca et l'atmosphère générale évoquent un «palazzo» italien.
Détail ci-dessous à droite: la salle de bains dessinée par Xavier Tronel, avec son sol carrelé en terre cuite. Le lavabo et la baignoire ont été insérés dans une pierre traitée à l'huile de lin. Les trois miroirs avec un cadre en bois de pin ajoutent encore à l'effet géométrique du décor.
Double page suivante: la chaleureuse cuisine, l'une des pièces maîtresses de la maison. Au centre, une grande table de ferme, dessinée par Patrice Nourissat et réalisée en pin teinté par un artisan de la région. C'est autour d'elle que s'assoient la famille et les amis pour des repas à la bonne franquette.

Oben und rechte Seite: zwei Ansichten des ocker und olivgrün gestrichenen Schlafzimmers. Der Wandfries erinnert an Piero della Francesca, die ganze Atmosphäre läßt an einen italienischen Palazzo denken.
Detail unten rechts: das von Xavier Tronel gestaltete Badezimmer mit Terrakotta-Bodenfliesen. Der Stein, aus dem die Waschbecken

und die Wanne geschnitten sind, wurde mit Leinöl behandelt. Die drei in Kiefer gerahmten Spiegel unterstreichen die graphische Ausdruckskraft des Raumes.
Folgende Doppelseite: die einladende Küche, einer der wichtigsten Räume des Hauses. Sie wurde von Patrice Nourissat entworfen und von einem hiesigen Handwerker in lasierter Kiefer gearbeitet. Beherrschendes Möbelstück ist der große Bauerntisch, an dem sich Familie und Freunde zu zwanglosen Mahlzeiten einfinden.

Above: the garden façade showing the turrets which were added in the 19th century.
Left: the pool and the poolhouse, both designed by Louis-Charles de Rémusat.

Ci-dessus: la façade côté jardin, avec ses tourelles rajoutées au XIXe siècle.
A gauche: la piscine et la cabine de bain, toutes deux dessinées par Louis-Charles de Rémusat.

Oben: die Gartenfassade mit den im 19. Jahrhundert hinzugefügten Ecktürmchen.
Links: der Swimmingpool mit dem Umkleidehäuschen, beides nach Entwürfen von Louis-Charles de Rémusat gebaut.

"My Father's Castle": Louis-Charles de Rémusat refers to the family property with an appropiate veiled reference to the title of one of Pagnol's best-loved books about Provence. The chateau is a splendid 18th-century construction that was acquired by the late father Rémusat just after the last war. With a rare sensibility he decided not to tear out the interiors but to leave all the 19th-century decoration, including wall hangings, upholstery and curtains, in place. Such a gesture of deference towards the building's gracious and aristocratic past has allowed the chateau, thus preserved, to age gracefully, as if lost in time. Louis-Charles, who trained as an architect, has restored and modernized the extensive outbuildings, making the property a real family home where the Rémusats all gather for Christmas and the long summer holidays.

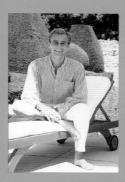

«Le château de mon père»

Cette allusion au titre de l'un des plus beaux romans de Pagnol sur la Provence prend tout son sens dans la bouche de Louis-Charles de Rémusat lorsqu'il parle de sa propriété de famille. Le château en question est une splendide demeure du XVIIIe siècle achetée par feu monsieur de Rémusat père juste après la dernière guerre. Avec une sensibilité rare, celui-ci a décidé de conserver la décoration du XIXe siècle, y compris tentures murales, tissus d'ameublement et rideaux. Grâce à ce respect pour son passé élégant et aristocratique, le château a gardé intact toute sa grâce d'autrefois. Louis-Charles, qui a une formation d'architecte, a restauré et modernisé les nombreuses dépendances, transformant la propriété en une véritable maison de famille où les Rémusat se retrouvent à chaque Noël et pour les grandes vacances.

»Das Schloß meines Vaters«: Louis-Charles de Rémusat bezeichnet seinen Familiensitz in Anlehnung an den Titel eines der beliebtesten Provence-Bände Marcel Pagnols augenzwinkernd als »Schloß meines Vaters«. Der Herrensitz ist ein prachtvolles Gebäude aus dem 18. Jahrhundert, das der verstorbene Monsieur Rémusat senior kurz nach dem zweiten Weltkrieg kaufte. Mit seltenem Feingefühl beschloß er, die Innenausstattung nicht herauszureißen, sondern die gesamte Dekoration aus dem 19. Jahrhundert einschließlich der Wandbehänge, Polster und Vorhänge beizubehalten. Dank solcher Ehrfurcht vor einer anmutigen, aristokratischen Vergangenheit war es dem Gebäude vergönnt, in Frieden zu altern, als sei es der Zeit entflohen. Louis-Charles, von Beruf Architekt, erneuerte und modernisierte die weitläufigen Nebengebäude und machte den Besitz zu einem echten Heim der Rémusats, in dem sich alle Familienmitglieder jedes Jahr zu Weihnachten und in den langen Sommerferien einfinden.

Louis-Charles' study, rather grandly referred to as the "Salle d'Armes", where the extensive collection of guns and trophies that belonged to his father, a great hunter, are exhibited. The wallpaper, which imitates wood, was part of the 19th-century decoration that came with the house.

Le bureau de Louis-Charles, appelé avec humour «la salle d'armes», car il abrite l'impressionnante collection de fusils et de trophées de son père, un grand chasseur. Le papier peint, en trompe-l'œil de bois, date du XIXe siècle.

Louis-Charles' recht großartig als »Fechtsaal« bezeichnetes Arbeitszimmer mit einer großen Sammlung von Waffen und Trophäen seines Vaters, eines passionierten Jägers. Die Tapete, eine Holznachbildung, war Teil der Ausstattung aus dem 19. Jahrhundert, die im Haus belassen wurde.

Below: the longest Louis XV sofa ever made, or known to be in existence, in front of the great bookcase in the billiard room. The floor is in
the local earthenwear "tomettes" tiles.
Detail right: a detail of the typically Provençal workmanship on the
doors.

Ci-dessous: le canapé Louis XV devant la grande bibliothèque de la
salle de billard est, à ce que l'on sache, le plus long jamais réalisé. Le
sol est recouvert des tomettes en terre cuite de la région.
Détail à droite: un détail des portes de la bibliothèque, de facture
typiquement provençale.

Unten: das längste Louis-XV-Sofa, das je gebaut wurde oder bekannt
ist, vor dem großen Bücherschrank im Billardzimmer. Der Fußboden
ist mit den ortstypischen irdenen »Tomettes« gefliest.
Detail rechts: ein Ausschnitt, der die typisch provenzalische Verarbei-
tung der Schranktüren zeigt.

Above: the blue bedroom on the first floor with its imposing bed "à la Polonaise". The chateau was decorated with a selection of chintz fabrics, well over a hundred years ago.
Facing page: The sun has faded the vibrant colours in the flowery "petit salon". The medallion over the door represents "summer" and is an 18th-century pastel.

Ci-dessus: la chambre bleue du premier étage, avec son imposant lit à la polonaise. Le vaste ensemble de chintz qui orne le château a été choisi au XIXe siècle.
Page de droite: le soleil a fané les couleurs vives du tissu fleuri du petit salon. Le médaillon au-dessus de la porte est un pastel du XVIIIe siècle représentant l'été.

Oben: das blaue Schlafzimmer im ersten Stock mit seinem mächtigen Himmelbett. Das Schloß wurde vor weit über hundert Jahren mit einer Auswahl an Chintzstoffen ausgestattet.
Rechte Seite: Von der Sonne sind die leuchtenden Farben des mit Blumenmotiven übersäten kleinen Salons verblaßt. Das Medaillon über der Tür, ein Pastellbild aus dem 18. Jahrhundert, zeigt eine Allegorie des Sommers.

An art dealer's home: A well-known New York art dealer and his wife have converted this classified building, which was probably originally a monastery, into a modern, minimalist refuge. They first spotted the place, which had been an 18th-century silkworm farm, in 1989 and were immediately seduced by its unusual proportions. Here, they felt, was a Provençal house unlike any other that could be the perfect home to display their important collection of contemporary art. They chose the architect Claudio Silvestrin, an Italian based in London, to adapt the structure to is new function. His work was essentially a quest for purity, respecting the proportions and the rustic appeal of the house. His influence is also to be felt in the monolithic treatment given to the swimming pool shown on the facing page. The façade, considered a national monument, was not to be changed in any way. The floor-length windows, which had been partly bricked up in the 19th century, provide the perfect, indirect lighting for displaying modern art.

La maison d'un marchand d'art

Ce bâtiment classé, à l'origine monastère devenu magnanerie au XVIIIe siècle, a été transformé en retraite moderne et minimaliste par un célèbre marchand d'art new-yorkais et sa femme. Ils ont été immédiatement séduits par ses proportions inhabituelles: cette demeure provençale unique en son genre allait faire un écrin idéal pour leur importante collection d'art contemporain. Ils ont demandé à Claudio Silvestrin, un architecte italien habitant à Londres, d'adapter la structure à sa nouvelle fonction. Ce dernier a cherché à épurer le bâtiment au maximum, respectant les volumes existants et l'attrait rustique de la maison. On retrouve également l'influence de Silvestrin dans l'aspect monolithique de la piscine que l'on peut voir sur la page de droite. La façade, classée Monument Historique, ne pouvait être modifiée mais ses hautes fenêtres partiellement murées de briques au dix-neuvième diffusaient déjà à l'intérieur une lumière indirecte convenant parfaitement aux œuvres d'art moderne.

Das Haus eines Kunsthändlers: Ein bekannter New Yorker Kunsthändler und seine Frau verwandelten dieses unter Denkmalschutz stehende Gebäude, vermutlich ursprünglich ein Kloster, in ein modernes, minimalistisch ausgestattetes Refugium. Sie entdeckten das Haus, das im 18. Jahrhundert zur Seidenraupenzucht genutzt wurde, im Jahr 1989 und waren sofort von seinen ausgefallenen Proportionen begeistert. Dies, erkannten sie, war ein provenzalisches Haus, das sich von allen anderen unterschied und in einen perfekten Rahmen für ihre bedeutende Sammlung moderner Kunst umgewandelt werden konnte. Als Architekten wählten sie den in London ansässigen Italiener Claudio Silvestrin, der das Gebäude seiner neuen Funktion anpassen sollte. Sein Konzept war vor allem größtmögliche Schlichtheit. Er behielt die Raumaufteilung bei und bewahrte so die rustikale Wirkung des Gebäudes. Sein Einfluß ist auch in der monolithischen Behandlung des rechts abgebildeten Swimmingpools zu spüren. Die als Nationaldenkmal eingestufte Fassade durfte zwar in keiner Weise verändert werden, doch geben die bis zu Boden reichenden Fenster, die im 19. Jahrhundert zum Teil zugemauert wurden, ein ideales Licht für die Präsentation der modernen Kunstobjekte.

On the previous pages: *the ground floor of the long, low building is one vast room, sparsely furnished, that sets off paintings and sculptures perfectly. The partly bricked-up windows are one of the buildings most interesting original features. The sculptures in the foreground are by Xawery Wolski, and the painting on the far wall is by Peter Joseph.*
Above: *the minimalist kitchen, where guests congregate in summer to help prepare Provençal picnics to be consumed "al fresco".*

Double page précédente: *le rez-de-chaussée du bâtiment long et bas n'est occupé que par une seule grande pièce peu meublée où tableaux et sculptures sont parfaitement mis en valeur. Les fenêtres partielle-ment murées avec des briques étaient l'un des aspects les plus intéres-sants du bâtiment. Les sculptures au premier plan sont de Xawery Wolski. Sur le mur du fond, une toile signée Peter Joseph.*
Ci-dessus: *la cuisine minimaliste où, l'été, les invités se rassemblent pour aider à préparer des pique-niques provençaux que l'on consomme ensuite à la fraiche.*

Vorhergehende Doppelseite: *Das Erdgeschoß in dem langgestreck-ten, niedrigen Gebäude besteht aus einem großen, spärlich eingerich-teten Raum, in dem die Bilder und Plastiken optimal zur Geltung kommen. Die teilweise zugemauerten Fenster sind eines der interes-santesten Originalelemente des Hauses. Die Skulpturen im Vorder-grund stammen von Xawery Wolsky, das Gemälde an der Rückwand von Peter Joseph.*
Oben: *die minimalistische Küche, in der sich im Sommer Gäste ein-finden, um bei der Vorbereitung provenzalischer Picknicks zu helfen, die anschließend unter freiem Himmel eingenommen werden.*

A simple pale oak dining-table designed by the architect Claudio Silvestrin pays homage to the long refractory tables of the monks who probably originally inhabited the house. The artwork in the background is by Maurizio Pellegrin. Throughout the house, modern art cohabits easily with the ancient structure, taking on a life of its own in the purity of the space.

Une simple table de salle à manger en chêne clair dessinée par l'architecte Claudio Silvestrin en hommage aux longues tables de réfectoire des moines, probablement les premiers occupants des lieux. Au mur, une œuvre de Maurizio Pellegrin. Partout dans la maison, des œuvres d'art moderne cohabitent avec bonheur avec la structure ancienne, la pureté des volumes architecturaux leur insufflant une vie nouvelle.

Ein schlichter heller Eßtisch aus Eiche, entworfen vom Architekten Claudio Silvestrin als Anspielung an die langen Refektoriumstische, an denen die wohl einst hier ansässigen Mönche gespeist haben dürften. Die Arbeit im Hintergrund stammt von Maurizio Pellegrin. Im ganzen Haus harmoniert moderne Kunst mit den alten architektonischen Elementen, nicht ohne in der Reinheit dieses Rahmens ein Eigenleben zu führen.

The solid stone sinks in the master bathroom. They are a true expression of Silvestrin's graphic approach to interiors. The pale stone and the white walls allow the strong Provençal light and the breathtaking view to become the real protagonists of the room.

Les lavabos en pierre massive de la grande salle de bains. Ils illustrent parfaitement le style géométrique de Silvestrin. La pierre pâle et les murs blancs s'effacent devant la belle lumière provençale et la vue somptueuse qui sont les véritables éléments du décor.

Die soliden steinernen Waschtische im Badezimmer zeigen Silvestrins graphischen Ansatz bei der Gestaltung von Innenräumen in aller Deutlichkeit. Der helle Stein und die weißen Wände verstärken noch das harte provenzalische Licht und die eindrucksvolle Aussicht, die eigentlichen Hauptelemente des Raumes.

Above and below: *two more views of the bathroom on the first floor, impressive in its simplicity. The extraordinary freestanding bath, carved out of stone, sits alone like a scooped-out fruit or an oversized shell and is the focal point of the room.*

Ci-dessus et ci-dessous: *la salle de bains du premier étage, d'une simplicité saisissante. L'extraordinaire baignoire sculptée dans la pierre repose sur le sol comme un fruit évidé ou un immense coquillage.*

Oben und unten: *zwei weitere Ansichten des in seiner Schlichtheit ausdrucksvollen Badezimmers im ersten Stock. Die ungewöhnlich freistehende Badewanne ist aus Stein gemeißelt und steht wie eine ausgehöhlte Fruchtschale oder eine überdimensionale Muschel ganz allein als optischer Brennpunkt mitten im Raum.*

One of Paris' most prominent modern art dealers and collectors,
Enrico Navarra, first made his entrée in the closed world of the top
galleries when he was a door-to-door salesman peddling calculators.
Apparently he was making such a good job of it that one of the dealers gave him a box of lithographs to push: he indeed sold them all,
and the rest, as they say, is history. In close collaboration with the architect Anezin, Navarra built his Provençal hideaway about fifteen
years ago. He knew exactly what he wanted: a simple, modernist
structure that would provide a backdrop to his collection of contemporary art. One small house soon proved insufficient to house
Navarra's many weekend guests, and so another was added: a loft-
like structure that houses only the master bedroom and the inside
pool.

Enrico Navarra

Grand marchand d'art et collectionneur parisien, Enrico Navarra a
fait son entrée dans le monde fermé des grandes galeries alors
qu'il était représentant de commerce, vendant des calculatrices de
porte à porte. Il était si convaincant qu'un galeriste lui confia un
jour un coffret de lithographies à vendre. Ils les écoula toutes
comme des petits pains. Le reste, comme on dit, appartient à l'histoire. En étroite collaboration avec l'architecte Anezin, Navarra a
fait construire sa retraite provençale il y a une quinzaine d'années.
Il savait exactement ce qu'il voulait: une structure simple et moderniste pouvant accueillir sa collection d'art contemporain. Une
première maison fut construite, mais elle s'avéra vite trop petite
pour recevoir tous les amis le week-end, aussi on y rajouta rapide-
ment une seconde structure de type loft qui n'accueille que la
chambre de maître et une piscine intérieure.

Enrico Navarra ist einer der prominentesten Pariser Händler und
Sammler moderner Kunst. Sein Debut in der geschlossenen Welt der
vornehmen Galerien gab er als Vertreter für Taschenrechner. Offenbar
machte er seine Sache gut, denn einer der Kunsthändler drückte ihm
einen Karton mit Lithographien in die Hand, die er an den Mann
bringen sollte. Er verkaufte sie restlos, und alles weitere ergab sich sozusagen von selbst. Seinen Zufluchtsort in der Provence baute
Navarra sich vor rund fünfzehn Jahren in enger Zusammenarbeit mit
dem Architekten Anezin. Er wußte ganz genau, was er wollte,
nämlich ein einfaches, modern wirkendes Gebäude, das die passende
Kulisse für seine Sammlung von Gegenwartskunst abgeben würde.
Das kleine Haus erwies sich bald als zu eng für Navarras zahlreiche
Wochenendgäste, deshalb wurde ein weiteres angebaut. Es entstand
ein hallenartiges Gebäude, das lediglich Navarras Schlafzimmer und
den Swimmingpool beherbergt.

Page 271: The giant red plantpot, a sculpted piece by Jean-Pierre Raynaud, dominates the grounds, a sculpture park showcasing some of Navarra's most important pieces.
Above: the salon in the guest-house. The piece on the left is by Le Gac. The round painting on the far wall is by Tom Wesselmann.
Facing page: the pool room. In the foreground a Le Corbusier "chaise-longue", in the background a piece of Oceanic primitive art, and a smaller sculpture by Raynaud.

Page 271: Un gigantesque pot de fleur, sculpture de Jean-Pierre Raynaud, domine la propriété, un parc de sculptures où sont exposées quelques-unes des plus belles pièces de Navarra.
Ci-dessus: le salon de la maison d'amis. Le tableau à gauche est de Le Gac. La toile ronde sur le mur du fond est signée Tom Wesselmann.
Page de droite: le coin «salon» de la piscine intérieure. Au premier plan, une chaise longue de Le Corbusier et au fond, une sculpture primitive océanienne et une autre, plus petite, de Raynaud.

Page 271: Der riesige rote Blumentopf ist eine Plastik Jean-Pierre Raynauds. Er beherrscht das Grundstück, das eigentlich ein Skulpturenpark mit einigen von Navarras bedeutendsten Stücken ist.
Oben: der Salon im Gästehaus. Das Werk links stammt von Le Gac. Das runde Gemälde an der rückwärtigen Wand ist ein Tom Wesselmann.
Rechte Seite: der Vorraum des Swimmingpools. Im Vordergrund eine Liege von Le Corbusier, im Hintergrund eine primitive Plastik aus Ozeanien und eine kleinere Arbeit von Raynaud.

Detail right: *the bed designed by Mario Botta with a monumental painting by Jean-Michel Basquiat as a headboard.*
Below: *a view of the "wall of images" in front of the bed in the master bedroom. The painting in the background is a Christo avant-project for the wrapping of the Reichstag.*

Détail de droite: *le lit dessiné par Mario Botta avec une peinture monumentale de Jean-Michel Basquiat en guise de tête de lit.*
Ci-dessous: *le «mur d'images» devant le lit de la chambre de maître. La peinture en arrière-plan est un avant-projet de Christo pour l'emballage du Reichstag.*

Detail rechts: *das von Mario Botta entworfene Bett, dem ein monumentales Gemälde von Jean-Michel Basquiat als Kopfteil dient.*
Unten: *ein Blick auf die »Bilderwand« vor dem Bett im Schlafzimmer. Das Gemälde im Hintergrund ist ein Vorentwurf von Christo für die Verhüllung des Berliner Reichstages.*

Above: *a view of the corridor, with the three-dimensional sculptures by Charles Simmonds niched in the wall itself. These are detailed miniature landscapes in mud, earth and tiny bricks, assembled by the artist on site with tweezers and other tools of the miniature trade.*
Following pages: *the indoor swimming pool, in "pietra serena", an Italian volcanic rock. The furniture is by Le Corbusier, and the room contains pieces by James Brown, Jenny Holzer and Raynaud. The statuettes are examples of primitive art.*

Ci-dessus: *le couloir, avec des sculptures tridimensionnelles de Charles Simmonds nichées directement dans le mur. Ces petits paysages faits avec de la boue, de la terre et de minuscules briques ont été assemblés sur place par l'artiste, avec des pinces à épiler et autres instruments de miniaturiste.*
Double page suivante: *la piscine intérieure en «pietra serena», une roche volcanique italienne. Les sièges sont de Le Corbusier. La salle abrite des œuvres de James Brown, Jenny Holzer et Raynaud, et des statuettes d'art primitif.*

Oben: *Blick in den Flur, wo Charles Simmonds dreidimensionale Plastiken direkt in die Wand eingearbeitet sind. Es handelt sich um detaillierte Miniaturlandschaften aus Schlamm, Erde und winzigen Ziegeln, die der Künstler an Ort und Stelle mit Hilfe einer Pinzette und anderer winziger Werkzeuge zusammengesetzt hat.*
Folgende Doppelseite: *Der Swimmingpool aus »pietra serena«, einem italienischen Vulkangestein. Die Sitzmöbel sind von Le Corbusier, darüber hinaus enthält der Raum Werke von James Brown, Jenny Holzer und Raynaud. Die Statuetten sind Beispiele primitiver Volkskunst.*

Not far from Saint-Paul-de-Vence, the picturesque hill village that has been Provence's leading artists' colony since the 1920s, lies a strictly contemporary "folie": the house of the painter and sculptor Arman. In his work, Arman has always exalted the object, transposing it from its proper place in our lives and thus transforming it into an object of art. When designing his house, he applied the same principle. Thus, strange and apparently unclassifiable items that on closer inspection turn out to be old and familiar friends such as springs, drums, telephones or sewing machines, have been used as building materials to produce a home which is a baffling challenge to conventional decorative principles. It might shock, it might charm or amuse, but this is one Provençal house that is light-years from the traditional country "mas".

Arman

Non loin de Saint-Paul-de-Vence, pittoresque village à flanc de colline devenu la plus importante colonie d'artistes de Provence dans les années vingt, se trouve une «folie» d'une modernité absolue: la maison du peintre et sculpteur Arman. Arman a toujours sublimé l'objet dans son œuvre, le sortant de son contexte pour en faire un «objet d'art». Pour concevoir sa maison, il a appliqué le même principe. Des objets étranges et apparemment inclassables, mais qui, vus de plus près, s'avèrent être de vieux compagnons familiers tels que ressorts, tambours, téléphones ou machines à coudre, ont servi de matériaux de construction, produisant un effet aux antipodes des principes conventionnels de la décoration. La maison peut choquer, charmer ou amuser, mais une chose est sûre: elle se situe à des années-lumière du «mas» provençal traditionnel.

Nicht weit entfernt von dem malerischen Bergdorf Saint-Paul-de-Vence, das seit den zwanziger Jahren als führende Künstlerkolonie der Provence gilt, steht das moderne, extravagante Haus des Malers und Bildhauers Arman. Bei seiner Arbeit geht es Arman stets um Objekte, die er ihrem alltäglichen Platz in unserem Leben entreißt und sie in Kunstwerke verwandelt. Bei der Planung seines Hauses wandte er dasselbe Verfahren an: Es wimmelt von eigenartigen, scheinbar undefinierbaren Dingen, die sich auf den zweiten Blick als gute alte Bekannte zu erkennen geben, seien es Sprungfedern, Waschmaschinentrommeln, Telefone oder Nähmaschinen. Sie sind Baumaterialien für ein Gebäude von verblüffender Eigenart, das konventionelle Dekorationsprinzipien auf den Kopf stellt. Mag man das Haus schockierend, ansprechend oder witzig finden, es ist jedenfalls meilenweit entfernt vom traditionellen provenzalischen Landhaus, dem »mas«.

Page 279: the summer dining-room, nicknamed the "Salon Mécanique" and mainly constructed from the insides of old washing machines and rusty cogs. The chairs on springs were originally tractor seats.
On the previous pages: an overall view of the house, among the luxuriant vegetation of the garden, with its façade in stainless steel washing machine drums. They reflect the heat and help keep the house cool in summer.
Above: the pool as seen from the roof with rusty butcher's scales.
Facing page and detail right: two aspects of the "telephone grotto".

Page 279: la salle à manger d'été, baptisée «le salon mécanique» et construite avec des tambours de machines à laver et des pignons rouillés. Les chaises à ressorts sont d'anciens sièges de tracteurs.
Double page précédente: une vue d'ensemble de la maison enfouie sous la végétation luxuriante du jardin, avec sa façade en acier trempé et en tambours de machines à laver. Le métal renvoie la chaleur et aide à conserver la maison fraîche pendant l'été.
Ci-dessus: la piscine vue du toit, décoré de vieilles balances.
Page et détail de droite: la «grotte téléphonique».

Seite 279: Der Sommer-Eßplatz, im Scherz auch »Salon mécanique« genannt, besteht überwiegend aus dem Innenleben ausgedienter Waschmaschinen und rostigen Zahnrädern. Die Hocker sind aus alten Traktorsitzen und großen Spiralfedern zusammengefügt.
Vorhergehende Doppelseite: Gesamtansicht des Hauses inmitten des üppig blühenden Gartens. Die Fassade wird von Waschmaschinentrommeln aus Edelstahl gebildet. Sie reflektieren die Hitze und halten das Haus im Sommer kühl.
Oben: Blick von dem mit verrosteten Fleischerwaagen ausstaffierten Dach auf den Swimmingpool.
Rechte Seite und Detail rechts: zwei Ansichten der »Telefongrotte«.

Above: The salon with its floor-length sliding windows and mirrored columns, features an Arman-designed sofa made from wooden shoe forms. On the left, a "throne" armchair fashioned by the artist out of a double-bass.
Detail right: part of an extensive collection of tribal art.

Ci-dessus: le salon avec ses baies vitrées et ses colonnes-miroirs, pour lequel Arman a conçu un canapé à partir d'embauchoirs en bois. A l'extrême gauche, un «trône» créé avec une contrebasse.
Détail de droite: quelques pièces de la grande collection d'art primitif.

Oben: Das Wohnzimmer ist mit durchgehenden Schiebetüren und verspiegelten Säulen versehen. Das von Arman selbst entworfene Sofa besteht aus hölzernen Schuhleisten. Links im Bild der »Thron«, ein vom Künstler persönlich aus einem Kontrabaß hergestellter Lehnstuhl.
Detail rechts: ein Teil einer umfangreichen Sammlung primitiver Kunst.

Detail right: a small sculpture in silver: a fractured vision of a tea tray and teapot.
Below: the inside dining-room, with more pieces from Arman's collection of primitive art. The piece on the wall is one of the celebrated "brush" paintings.

Détail de droite: une petite sculpture en argent, vision fragmentée d'un plateau à thé et sa théière.
Ci-dessous: la salle à manger intérieure, qui accueille d'autres pièces de la collection d'art primitif. Au mur, l'une des célèbres «peintures-brosse».

Detail rechts: eine kleine Plastik aus Silber: ein zerlegtes Tablett mit Teekanne.
Unten: das Eßzimmer mit weiteren Stücken aus Armans Sammlung primitiver Kunst. Die Wanddekoration ist eines der bekannten »Streichbürsten«-Bilder.

The mounted postman: In the sloping hills behind Vence lies the un-expected hideaway of the "Facteur à cheval", Jean-Pierre Roger, so named because he is the local postman and sometimes delivers the letters on horseback. A real rolling stone, he has had an adventurous life, which includes being chased by the "gendarmes" after eloping to Rome with his girlfriend – he was fourteen and a half at the time! Since then he has had quite a career as a motobike racer, but after a major accident Roger decided to settle down to work as a postman. His home, one of the numerous outbuildings on a large property, is said to have once been the local pottery. He has transformed it into a fairy-tale grotto, a mecca for lovers of all that is kitsch. The inside is entirely done in plaster, with the furniture built in as part of the structure. This, he says, is to confound the bailiffs – there is nothing to be taken away!

Le facteur à cheval

La surprenante retraite de Jean-Pierre Roger est cachée dans les collines qui s'étirent derrière Vence. Baptisé le «facteur à cheval» parce qu'il livre parfois le courrier sur sa monture, Jean-Pierre est un aventurier dans l'âme: à quatorze ans et demi, il était déjà recherché par les gendarmes après s'être enfui à Rome avec sa petite amie! Depuis, il a fait une belle carrière de champion de courses de motos jusqu'à ce qu'un grave accident le convainque d'adopter la vie plus tranquille d'employé des postes. Sa maison, l'une des nombreuses dépendances d'une grande propriété, semble avoir été autrefois la poterie locale. Il l'a transformée en grotte féérique, un sanctuaire pour les amoureux du kitsch. L'inté-rieur est entièrement revêtu de plâtre, les meubles étant intégrés dans la structure. Ainsi, déclare-t-il, les huissiers peuvent toujours venir, ils ne pourront rien emporter!

»Der berittene Briefträger«: In den sanften Hügeln hinter Vence liegt völlig unerwartet der Zufluchtsort des »Facteur à cheval« Jean-Pierre Roger, der so genannt wird, weil er in dieser Gegend für das Austragen der Post zuständig ist und dies gelegentlich vom Pferderücken aus tut. Im Laufe seines bewegten Lebens lernte er alle Höhen und Tiefen kennen. Er wurde sogar einmal von den Gendarmen verfolgt, als er mit seiner Freundin nach Rom durchbrannte – schließlich war er da-mals erst vierzehneinhalb! Später machte Roger Karriere als Motor-rad-Rennfahrer, sagte dem Rennsport jedoch nach einem schweren Unfall Lebewohl und arbeitet seither als Briefträger. Sein Haus, eines von zahlreichen kleinen Gebäuden auf einem weitläufigen Gelände, soll früher einmal die örtliche Töpferei gewesen sein. Jean-Pierre Roger hat es in eine Märchenhöhle verwandelt, ein Mekka für jeden, der Kitsch in jeglicher Form liebt. Das Innere ist vollständig aus Gips, auch die Möbel sind komplett integriert. Das soll, wie er sagt, den Gerichtsvollzieher verwirren, denn so kann er schließlich nichts weg-pfänden ...

On the previous pages: the dining-room with the oval table, curved
bench and sideboard, all immovable parts of the structure. The mural
painting is by Gaby Blum.
Above: the bedroom, with a collection of souvenirs from Roger's
travels.
Facing page: the entrance, showing the artisanal aspect of the
plaster work.
On the following pages: the organically shaped living room, to which
the illuminated fish tank gives a slightly futuristic air.

Double page précédente: la salle à manger, avec sa table ovale,
son banc arrondi et son buffet, le tout inamovible. La fresque est de
Gaby Blum.
Ci-dessus: la chambre à coucher, décorée avec des souvenirs de
voyage.
Page de droite: l'entrée, où apparaît l'aspect rugueux du plâtre brut.
Double page suivante: le salon aux formes organiques, auquel
l'aquarium illuminé confère un air légèrement futuriste.

Vorhergehende Doppelseite: Das Eßzimmer mit dem ovalen Tisch,
der gebogenen Sitzbank und der Anrichte ist aus einem Guß und
unverrückbarer Teil der Struktur. Das Wandgemälde stammt von
Gaby Blum.
Oben: das Schlafzimmer mit einer Sammlung von Souvenirs,
die Roger von seinen Reisen mitgebracht hat.
Rechte Seite: Der Dielenbereich zeigt die handwerkliche Qualität der
Gipsarbeiten.
Folgende Doppelseite: das organisch geformte Wohnzimmer, dem
ein beleuchtetes Aquarium eine leicht futuristische Note verleiht.

The studio of Jacques Henri Lartigue: consecrated as one of the most illustrious photographers of the 20th century, Jacques Henri Lartigue believed his true talent was for painting. Indeed, his photography was only really discovered in 1963, when he was already sixty-nine. Until then it had remained a private, albeit time-consuming, hobby. For most of his life, he worked as a painter. His third wife, Florette, still lives in their cottage in Provence that he baptized "Dinky Soleil": the nickname he invented for his father-in-law. A rural retreat, reflecting Lartigue's sunny personality, the cottage is full of knick-knacks evoking their life together. Next door is his studio, untouched since his death, reflects his simple tastes and the relentless romanticism that led him to write "Je t'aime" over and over again on a canvas of brilliantly coloured flowers for his wife.

L'atelier de Jacques Henri Lartigue

Consacré l'un des plus grands photographes du XXe siècle, Jacques Henri Lartigue se considérait avant tout comme un peintre. Il avait déjà soixante-neuf ans lorqu'on a commencé à s'intéresser à ses photos, qui n'étaient pour lui qu'un passe-temps quelque peu envahissant. Il a passé la plus grande partie de sa vie à peindre. Florette, sa troisième femme, vit toujours dans leur petite maison de Provence, baptisée «Dinky Soleil»: un surnom qu'il inventa pour son beau-père. Ce refuge de campagne, qui reflète la nature chaleureuse de Lartigue, regorge de bibelots évoquant leur vie à deux. Tout près de là, son atelier, resté intact depuis sa mort, témoigne de son goût simple et de l'incorrigible romantisme qui l'a incité à écrire «Je t'aime» encore et encore sur une toile couverte de fleurs vivement colorées destinée à sa femme.

Auch wenn er unumstritten als einer der besten Photographen des 20. Jahrhunderts gilt, war Jacques Henri Lartigue selbst der Meinung, sein eigentliches Talent liege in der Malerei. Sein photographisches Werk wurde nämlich erst 1963 bekannt, als er bereits neunundsechzig Jahre alt war. Bis dahin war die Photographie für ihn ein zwar zeitaufwendiges, doch rein privates Hobby gewesen. Die meiste Zeit seines Lebens arbeitete er als Maler. Seine dritte Frau Florette lebt noch heute in dem gemeinsamen Bauernhaus in der Provence, das er »Dinky Soleil« taufte – ein Spitzname, den er sich für seinen Schwiegervater ausgedacht hatte. Das abgelegene Häuschen atmet noch Lartigues sonniges Gemüt und ist vollgestopft mit Nippes aus der gemeinsamen Zeit. Gleich nebenan liegt sein Atelier, das seit seinem Tod unangetastet blieb. Es zeugt von seinem unprätentiösen Geschmack und seiner unverbesserlichen romantischen Ader, die ihn bewog, unzählige Male »Je t'aime« auf ein Bild mit leuchtend bunten Blumen zu schreiben, das er seiner Frau widmete.

Above and facing page: *two views of Lartigue's painting studio. The folding campbed and gay patchwork quilt, and indeed the simplicity with which the whole house is furnished, do not betray Lartigue's wealthy origins. The walls were painted at random in a swirling, colourful pattern. In fact, Lartigue used the wall to clean his paintbrush everytime he took a break. Florette vowed to keep the studio intact and indeed no changes have been made since Lartigue's death.*

Ci-dessus et page de droite: *l'atelier de Lartigue. Comme le décor humble de la maison attenante, le lit de camp et l'édredon en patchwork aux couleurs gaies ne témoignent pas des origines aisées de Lartigue. Les murs ont été peints à grands coups de pinceaux dans un tourbillon de couleurs. Pendant ses pauses, Lartigue y essuyait même ses pinceaux. Florette s'est promis de conserver cet atelier tel quel et, de fait, rien n'a changé depuis la mort de l'artiste.*

Oben und rechte Seite: *zwei Ansichten von Lartigues Atelier. Das Feldbett mit der fröhlichen Patchworkdecke und vor allem die Schlichtheit, mit der das ganze Haus eingerichtet ist, täuschen über Lartigues wohlhabende Herkunft hinweg. Die Wände sind nach dem Zufallsprinzip mit wirbelnden bunten Mustern bemalt. Lartigue strich nämlich an der Wand seine Pinsel ab, bevor er Pause machte. Florette versprach, das Atelier unangetastet zu lassen, und so ist seit Lartigues Tod nicht das geringste daran verändert worden.*

Adresses et sélection de brocantes
Adresses and selected "brocantes"
Adressen und ausgewählte »Brocantes«

Château d'Ansouis
Museum
Résidence des Ducs de
Sabran-Pontevès
84240 Ansouis

Henri Aubanel-Baroncelli
Horse Riding
Lou Simbèu
Route d'Aigues-Mortes,
Clos du Rhône
13460 Les Saintes-Maries-
de-la-Mer

**Anna Bonde &
Arne Tengblad**
Decoration
Quartier Bel Air
84220 Goult

Marie-Christine Cagnolari
Vineyard
Domaine de Souviou
RN 8
83330 Le Beausset

Bruno Carles
Shop
209–235 avenue de Lattre
de Tassigny
34400 Lunel

Denis Colomb
Architecture & Design
8 place Adolphe Max
75008 Paris

Denys Colomb de Daunant
Hotel
Le Mas de Cacharel
13460 Les Saintes-Maries-
de-la-Mer

Nasrine Faghih
Architecture
3 rue Chapon
75003 Paris

Emile Garcin
Estate Agency
8 boulevard Mirabeau
13210 Saint-Rémy-de-
Provence

Jacques Grange
Interior Decoration
118 rue du Faubourg-
St.-Honoré
75008 Paris

Michel Klein
Fashion
6 rue du Prè-aux-Clercs
75007 Paris

Enrico Navarra
Modern Art Gallery
16 avenue Matignon
75008 Paris

Xavier Nicod
Antiques
9 avenue des Quatre
Otages
84800 L'Isle-sur-la-Sorgue

Gerald Pellen
Horse Breeding
Mas les grandes Bouisses
13150 Boulbon

**Jennifer &
Jean-Marie Rocchia**
Provençal Honey and
Truffels
Campagne le Prince
13100 Beaurecueil

Château Unang
Hotel
Marie-Hélène &
Jean-Albert Lefer
Route de Méthanis
84570 Malemort-du-
Comtat

"Brocante" shops:

Fan'Broc
22 boulevard Mirabeau
Saint-Rémy-de-Provence

Philippe Eckert
Ebène
38 boulevard Victor Hugo
Saint-Rémy-de-Provence

Sous L'Olivier
7 boulevard Mirabeau
Saint-Rèmy-de-Provence

Catherine & Michel Biehn
Espace Béchard
1 avenue Jean Charmasson
L'Isle-sur-la-Sorgue

Christine &
Denis Nossereau
7 avenue des Quatre
Otages
L'Isle-sur-la-Sorgue

Hervé Baume
19 rue de la Petite-Fusterie
Avignon

Hôtel Nord-Pinus
6 rue du Palais
Arles

"Brocante" markets:

Arles: Boulevard des Lices
el primer miercoles del mes
il primo mercredi del mese
primeira quarta-feira do
mês

Avignon: Place Crillon
sábados por la mañana
tutti i sabati mattina
sábados de manhã
Place des Carmes
domingos por la mañana
tutte le domeniche mattina
domingos de manha

L'Isle-sur-la-Sorgue:
Avenue des Quatre Otages
sábados y domingos
sabato e domenica
sábados e domingos

Marseille: Cours Julien el
segundo domingo del mes
la seconda domenica del
mese segundo domingo
do mês

Bibliographie / Bibliography

Agulhon, Maurice: *The Republic in the Village. The People of the Var from the French Revolution to the Second Republic*, Cambridge, 1982

Aubanel, Henri: *Je suis Manadier*, Editions du Conquistador, 1957

Bicknell, C.: *The Prehistoric Rock Engravings in the Italian Maritime Alps*, Bordighera, 1902

Borgé, Jacques, and Nicolas Viasnoff: *Archives de Provence*, Editions Michèle Trinkville, 1994

Chabot, Jacques: *La Provence de Giono*, Aix-en-Provence, 1982

Curnier, Pierre: *La Haute-Provence dans les lettres françaises*, Chantemerle Editeur, 1973

D'Agay, Frédéric: *La Provence des châteaux et des bastides*, Editions du Chêne, 1991

David, Elizabeth: *French Provincial Cooking*, London, 1960

Desaule, Pierre: *Les Bories de Vaucluse*, Paris, 1976

Deux, Pierre, Pierre Moulin, Pierre Le Vec and Linda Dannenberg: *L'Art de vivre en Provence*, Flammarion, 1987

Durrell, Lawrence: *Caesar's Vast Ghost*, faber and faber, 1990

Eydoux, Henri-Paul: *Promenades en Provence*, Editions André Balland, 1969

Lady Fortescue: *Perfume from Provence*, London, 1935

Ford, Ford Madox: *Provence. From Minstrels to the Machine*, London, 1935

Giono, Jean: *Provence*, Paris, 1957

— *Provence perdue*, Paris, 1967

Hare, Augustus: *The Rivieras*, London, 1897

Hennessy, James Pope: *Aspects of Provence*, London, 1952

Hughes, John: *An Itinerary in Provence and the Rhône*, London, 1822

Jacobs, Michael: *A Guide to Provence*, Penguin, 1988

James, Henry: *A Little Tour in France*, Penguin Travel Library, 1985

Jouveau, R.: *Histoire du Félibrige*, 1976

Legré, L.: *Le Poète Théodore Aubanel*, *Récit d'un témoin de sa vie*, Paris, 1984

Magnan, Pierre, and Daniel Faure: *Les Promenades de Jean Giono*, Editions du Chêne, 1994

Massot, J.-L.: *Maisons rurales et vie paysanne en Provence*, Ivry, 1975

Mauron, Marie: *Quand la Provence nous est contée*, Presses Pocket, 1975

Merimée, Prosper: *Notes d'un voyage dans le Midi de France*, Paris, 1835

Mermod, Françoise: *La Provence. Peintres et écrivains de Théophile Gautier à Paul Valéry, de Corot à Dufy*, Edition Mermod, 1956

Mistral, Frédéric: *Memoirs of Mistral*, London, 1907

Mouriès, Nathalie: *Guide Provence de charme*, Editions Rivage, 1994

Pagnol, Marcel: *La Gloire de mon père*, Paris, 1957

— *Le Château de ma mère*, Paris, 1958

— *Le Temps des secrets*, Paris, 1960

Pickvance, R.: *Van Gogh in Arles*, New York, 1984

Olivier-Elliot, Patrick: *Lubéron, carnets d'un voyageur attentif*, Editions Edisud, 1991

Petrarch: *L'Ascension du Mont Ventoux*, Editions Séquences, 1990

Reboul, J.-B.: *La Cuisinière provençale*, Marseille, 1895

Silvester, Hans, and Jean-Paul Clébert: *Tsiganes et gitanes*, Editions du Chêne, 1974

Stendhal: *Journal d'un voyage dans le midi de France*, Paris, 1858

Sussex, R.T.: *Henri Bosco: A Study of the Novels*, London, 1966

Vergé, Roger: *Cuisine of the Sun*, London, 1979

Remerciements / Acknowledgements / Danksagungen

This book would not have been possible without the help of my friends and advisors Anna Davenport, Elisabeth Kime and Kathy Korvin who all contributed greatly to the project.

Erica Lennard, Denis Colomb, Phillipe Seuillet, Jacques Grange, Marianne Haas, Nicholas Barrera, Nicole de Vesian, Marie-Colette and Jean Michel Borgeaud, Marie-Madeleine Nelson, Marilse de Font-Reaulx and especially Guilleaume de Laubier made the production of this book a reality with their help and advice.

The following stylists and magazines deserve credit for their productions which they kindly allowed us to reproduce: Bruno Carles was styled by Christine Grange-Bary for "Maison et Jardin"; Guillemette Goëlff was styled by Florence Beaufre; Michel Klein was styled by Marie Dahadie for "Maison et Jardin"; Xavier Nicod was styled by Anne-Marie Comte for "Marie Claire Maison"; Jacques Henri Lartigue was styled by Bibi Gex for "Elle Deco"; Arne Tengblad, Daniel Vial, Lillian Williams, Enrico Navarra, Arman and Le facteur à cheval were styled by Philippe Seuillet. The text background for La maison d'un marchand d'art came from Christine Lippens. Nicole de Vesian was styled by Sonia Dieudonné for "Maison et Jardin"; Le château de mon père was styled by Chris O'Byrne; Christiane et Serge Cagnolari was styled by Christine Grange-Bary for "Maison et Jardin", Nasrine Faghih was styled byGilles Dalliers for "Maison Française"; Franck Pascal et Marc Heracle was styled by Joëlle Balaresque for "Maison et Jardin".

Special thanks to Charles-Henri de L. for helping me with the manuscript in its final stages and for creating the conditions in which I could write.

This book is for my mother who first awoke my love of Provence.

Lisa Lovatt-Smith

Interior Design

Angelika Taschen / a.taschen@taschen.com

"A backbreaking photographic survey of African interiors."
—*Icon*, London, on *Inside Africa*

"Tout est dit dans ces images qui nous font visiter l'Afrique dans sa splendeur et sa pluralité."
—*Le Figaro*, Paris, on *Inside Africa*

INSIDE AFRICA
Ed. Angelika Taschen / Photos: Deidi von Schaewen / Hardcover, 2 volumes, format: 24 x 31.6 cm (9.4 x 12.4 in.), 912 pp. /
€ 99.99 / $ 125.99 / £ 69.99 / ¥ 15.000

BERLIN INTERIORS
Ed. Angelika Taschen / Ingeborg Wiensowski / Photos: Eric Laignel / Hardcover, format: 24 x 31.6 cm (9.4 x 12.4 in.), 320 pp.
€ 29.99 / $ 39.99 / £ 24.99 / ¥ 5.900

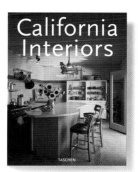

CALIFORNIA INTERIORS
Ed. Angelika Taschen / Diane Dorrans Saeks / Hardcover, format: 24 x 31.6 cm (9.4 x 12.4 in.), 304 pp.
€ 29.99 / $ 39.99 / £ 24.99 / ¥ 5.900

LONDON INTERIORS
Ed. Angelika Taschen / Jane Edwards / Hardcover, format: 24 x 31.6 cm (9.4 x 12.4 in.), 304 pp.
€ 29.99 / $ 39.99 / £ 24.99 / ¥ 5.900

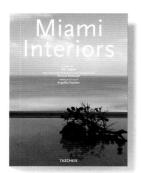

MIAMI INTERIORS
Ed. Angelika Taschen / Patricia Parinejad / Photos: Eric Laignel / Hardcover, format: 24 x 31.6 cm (9.4 x 12.4 in.), 320 pp.
€ 29.99 / $ 39.99 / £ 24.99 / ¥ 5.900

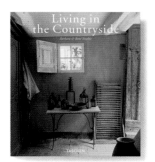

Interior Design

Angelika Taschen / a.taschen@taschen.com

LIVING IN THE COUNTRYSIDE
Ed. Angelika Taschen / Barbara & René Stoeltie /
Hardcover, format: 26 x 30.2 cm (10.2 x 11.9 in.),
400 pp.
€ 19.99 / $ 29.99 / £ 14.99 / ¥ 4.900

LIVING IN GREECE
Ed. Angelika Taschen / Barbara & René Stoeltie /
Hardcover, format: 26 x 30.2 cm (10.2 x 11.9 in.),
200 pp.
€ 19.99 / $ 29.99 / £ 14.99 / ¥ 4.900

*"…great pictures of
simple interiors, clean lines
and splashes of colour."*
—*The Times*, London, on *Living in Greece*

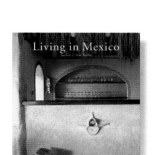

LIVING IN IRELAND
Ed. Angelika Taschen / Barbara & René Stoeltie /
Hardcover, format: 26 x 30.2 cm (10.2 x 11.9 in.),
200 pp.
€ 19.99 / $ 29.99 / £ 14.99 / ¥ 4.900

LIVING IN MEXICO
Ed. Angelika Taschen / Barbara & René Stoeltie /
Hardcover, format: 26 x 30.2 cm (10.2 x 11.9 in.),
200 pp.
€ 19.99 / $ 29.99 / £ 14.99 / ¥ 4.900

LIVING IN MOROCCO
Ec. Angelika Taschen / Barbara & René Stoeltie /
Hardcover, format: 26 x 30.2 cm (10.2 x 11.9 in.),
280 pp.
€ 19.99 / $ 29.99 / £ 14.99 / ¥ 4.900

New edition!

COUNTRY INTERIORS
Ed. Angelika Taschen / Diane Dorrans Saeks /
Flexi-cover, format: 19.6 x 25.8 cm (7.7 x 10.1 in.),
304 pp.
€ 14.99 / $ 19.99 / £ 9.99 / ¥ 2.900

INDIAN INTERIORS
Ed. Angelika Taschen / Sunil Sethi / Photos: Deidi von
Schaewen / Hardcover, format: 19.6 x 25.8 cm
(7.7 x 10.1 in.), 320 pp.
€ 14.99 / $ 19.99 / £ 9.99 / ¥ 2.900

MOROCCAN INTERIORS
Ed. Angelika Taschen / Lisa Lovatt-Smith /
Flexi-cover, format: 19.6 x 25.8 cm
(7.7 x 10.1 in.), 320 pp.
€ 14.99 / $ 19.99 / £ 9.99 / ¥ 2.900

MOUNTAIN INTERIORS
Ed. Angelika Taschen / Beate Wedekind / Hardcover,
format: 19.6 x 25.8 cm (7.7 x 10.1 in.), 288 pp.
€ 14.99 / $ 19.99 / £ 9.99 / ¥ 2.900

NEW YORK INTERIORS
Ed. Angelika Taschen / Beate Wedekind / Hardcover,
format: 19.6 x 25.8 cm (7.7 x 10.1 in.), 288 pp.
€ 14.99 / $ 19.99 / £ 9.99 / ¥ 2.900

PARIS INTERIORS
Lisa Lovatt-Smith / Flexi-cover, format: 19.6 x 25.8 cm
(7.7 x 10.1 in.), 320 pp.
€ 14.99 / $ 19.99 / £ 9.99 / ¥ 2.900

SEASIDE INTERIORS
Ed. Angelika Taschen / Diane Dorrans Saeks / Flexi-cover,
format: 19.6 x 25.8 cm (7.7 x 10.1 in.), 304 pp.
€ 14.99 / $ 19.99 / £ 9.99 / ¥ 2.900

TUSCANY INTERIORS
Ed. Angelika Taschen / Paolo Rinaldi / Flexi-cover,
format: 19.6 x 25.8 cm (7.7 x 10.1 in.), 288 pp.
€ 14.99 / $ 19.99 / £ 9.99 / ¥ 2.900

Rhône

Orange

Avignon

Plateau de Vau

Nîmes

Tarascou

Apt

Luberé

Montpellier

Alpilles

Arles

Aigues-Mortes

Camargue

Ta

Aix

Les-saintes-Maries-
de-la-Mer

Marseille

Golfe du Lion

Méditè